Calvinism: A Very Short Introduction

VERY SHORT INTRODUCTIONS are for anyone wanting a stimulating and accessible way into a new subject. They are written by experts, and have been translated into more than 40 different languages.

The series began in 1995, and now covers a wide variety of topics in every discipline. The VSI library now contains over 450 volumes—a Very Short Introduction to everything from Psychology and Philosophy of Science to American History and Relativity—and continues to grow in every subject area.

Very Short Introductions available now:

ACCOUNTING Christopher Nobes
ADOLESCENCE Peter K. Smith
ADVERTISING Winston Fletcher
AFRICAN AMERICAN RELIGION
    Eddie S. Glaude Jr
AFRICAN HISTORY John Parker and
    Richard Rathbone
AFRICAN RELIGIONS Jacob K. Olupona
AGEING Nancy A. Pachana
AGNOSTICISM Robin Le Poidevin
AGRICULTURE Paul Brassley and
    Richard Soffe
ALEXANDER THE GREAT
    Hugh Bowden
ALGEBRA Peter M. Higgins
AMERICAN HISTORY Paul S. Boyer
AMERICAN IMMIGRATION
    David A. Gerber
AMERICAN LEGAL HISTORY
    G. Edward White
AMERICAN POLITICAL HISTORY
    Donald Critchlow
AMERICAN POLITICAL PARTIES
    AND ELECTIONS L. Sandy Maisel
AMERICAN POLITICS
    Richard M. Valelly
THE AMERICAN PRESIDENCY
    Charles O. Jones
THE AMERICAN REVOLUTION
    Robert J. Allison
AMERICAN SLAVERY
    Heather Andrea Williams
THE AMERICAN WEST Stephen Aron
AMERICAN WOMEN'S HISTORY
    Susan Ware

ANAESTHESIA Aidan O'Donnell
ANARCHISM Colin Ward
ANCIENT ASSYRIA Karen Radner
ANCIENT EGYPT Ian Shaw
ANCIENT EGYPTIAN ART AND
    ARCHITECTURE Christina Riggs
ANCIENT GREECE Paul Cartledge
THE ANCIENT NEAR EAST
    Amanda H. Podany
ANCIENT PHILOSOPHY Julia Annas
ANCIENT WARFARE Harry Sidebottom
ANGELS David Albert Jones
ANGLICANISM Mark Chapman
THE ANGLO-SAXON AGE John Blair
THE ANIMAL KINGDOM
    Peter Holland
ANIMAL RIGHTS David DeGrazia
THE ANTARCTIC Klaus Dodds
ANTISEMITISM Steven Beller
ANXIETY Daniel Freeman and
    Jason Freeman
THE APOCRYPHAL GOSPELS
    Paul Foster
ARCHAEOLOGY Paul Bahn
ARCHITECTURE Andrew Ballantyne
ARISTOCRACY William Doyle
ARISTOTLE Jonathan Barnes
ART HISTORY Dana Arnold
ART THEORY Cynthia Freeland
ASIAN AMERICAN HISTORY
    Madeline Y. Hsu
ASTROBIOLOGY David C. Catling
ASTROPHYSICS James Binney
ATHEISM Julian Baggini
AUGUSTINE Henry Chadwick

Jon Balserak

CALVINISM

A Very Short Introduction

OXFORD
UNIVERSITY PRESS

Great Clarendon Street, Oxford, OX2 6DP,
United Kingdom

Oxford University Press is a department of the University of Oxford.
It furthers the University's objective of excellence in research, scholarship,
and education by publishing worldwide. Oxford is a registered trade mark of
Oxford University Press in the UK and in certain other countries

Published in the United States of America by Oxford University Press
198 Madison Avenue, New York, NY 10016, United States of America

British Library Cataloguing in Publication Data
Data available

Library of Congress Control Number: 2016947627

ISBN 978-0-19-875371-1

Printed and bound by
CPI Group (UK) Ltd, Croydon, CR0 4YY

Contents

Preface

Books about Calvinism generally fall into one of two categories: those that seek to defend or attack its truthfulness and those that provide a detailed history of it. This study does not do either but instead explores some of the main ideas associated with Calvinism.

Calvinism embraces an impressive collection of ideas. During its roughly 500-year existence, it has had to adapt as it moved into different countries, and has consequently grown more diverse, covering not only theology but also terrain associated with politics, psychology, philosophy, the sciences, and the arts.

But Calvinism is also diverse in another way. This may be introduced by considering the common, and slightly humorous, question: was Calvin a Calvinist? The question is wrongheaded for several reasons, some of which help reveal Calvinism's breadth and variety. The main reason is that it works on the premise that Calvinism sprung from the mind of John Calvin alone (and thus it would be comical if *he*, of all people, were not considered a Calvinist), but that is simply not the case. It sprung, and is still springing, from many different sources. Thus, Calvinism, despite its name, has always been more than the thought of one man, such that it could at least hypothetically be the case that, depending on how we defined Calvinism, Calvin himself would hold a tenuous relationship to it.

This raises the issue of definition and, also, nomenclature. Calvinism. Reformed theology. The doctrines of grace. Five point Calvinism, also known through the acronym TULIP. Covenant theology (or Federalism). Neo-Calvinism (or Kuyperianism). Neo-orthodoxy. Neo-Puritanism. The New Calvinism. Etc. All these terms relate broadly to the same thing, but are not identical in terms of their referents. Some refer, for instance, to an understanding of Christian salvation, as is the case with TULIP. But others are broader. In this book, I will refer most often to 'Calvinism' and 'Reformed theology,' using them as if they were interchangeable, though I concede they are not, at least not in every case. The other phrases will be discussed, or at least mentioned, in various places throughout the book. Very little will be said on Neo-orthodoxy given how different it is from other expressions of Reformed thought.

But we have not dealt with the issue of definition sufficiently yet. Here things become difficult. The fact is that Calvinism is very hard to define. It's certainly impossible to define in a non-controversial manner. This has been true since the 16th century.

Many say, and perhaps with some justification, that the best way to define Calvinism is by looking at Reformed confessional statements, which set out the essential religious beliefs of those self-identifying as 'Reformed'. But this approach is not foolproof, as some of the confessions are so lengthy and detailed that they raise problems of their own related to how they ought to be interpreted. This is particularly true of the *Westminster Confession of Faith*, drawn up in 1646 as part of the Westminster standards by theologians who met at Westminster Abbey to produce new doctrinal standards for the Church of England, though these documents would end up being adopted by most Presbyterian churches throughout the world.

Nor is it clear how much of a Reformed confession needs to be believed for someone to be legitimately called a Calvinist? Why, for instance, can a Baptist be a Calvinist but not a Roman

Catholic? The answer cannot be found in their views on the sacraments, since Baptists do not agree with most Calvinists on baptizing infants. If the answer has to do with their doctrine of salvation, then we must ask: should Richard Baxter, who of course wrote *The Reformed Pastor* (1656), be considered Reformed? His theology strays, on major salvation-oriented issues like justification and the atonement, quite far from most Reformed confessions. Perhaps the answer has to do with church polity (i.e. government), but both Catholics and Baptists differ here too from most Calvinists, since most Calvinists hold to a Presbyterian form of church government. Besides, we might ask: can someone who believes every word of the *Savoy Declaration* be considered Reformed, since it differs with the *Westminster Confession of Faith* on essentially only the topic of polity—the *Savoy Declaration* having been prepared in 1658 by English Congregationalists, included Thomas Goodwin, John Owen, Philip Nye, and William Greenhill, who met at Savoy Palace in London?

Nor (again) is it clear which confessions rightly represent the Reformed position. There are, after all, many confessions and they do not all teach the same thing on all points. The *Heidelberg Catechism*, authored principally by Zacharias Ursinus and published in 1563, contains a discussion of the Christian Sabbath that some claim diverges from, say, the *Westminster*. There are others who think the two are essentially identical on the Sabbath—which nicely demonstrates the controversy to which I pointed earlier. What of other confessions? Should John Gill's *1729 Goat Yard Declaration of Faith* be included? Should a Baptist work like the *1689 Baptist Confession of Faith* be included? Should the *Thirty-nine Articles* be included? Article XXI of the *Thirty-nine* teaches (in its original edition of 1563, which was produced under the direction of the then-Archbishop of Canterbury, Matthew Parker) that general councils of the church cannot be called without the command of the civil authorities. Is this enough to disqualify it from inclusion among Reformed confessions?

The problem with all of these questions is that there is no definitive rationale that can be used for answering them. The moment someone tries to lay down a rationale, they simply become part of the process of diversification of the Reformed tradition that has been going on for centuries.

At this point, we may wonder whether there might be other ways to approach the work of defining Reformed theology. Perhaps there are. But it's very difficult. It's like defining the Labour Party or the Republican Party. It's even, to look from a different perspective, a little bit like trying to set boundaries on the English language. It has changed as it has been adopted by other countries. Moreover, each new generation places their own individual stamp on it, and the process meets with both protest and approval.

Now to be sure, the work of defining Calvinism depends on the interests the definer brings with them. A Christian minister is likely to be interested in finding a standard set of doctrines that can serve as a model for his church members; and that is entirely understandable and admirable. A historian, on the other hand, is probably going to focus on other concerns and, quite likely, will be more interested in development, diversity, and ambiguity. And it is this latter approach that characterizes my own. I don't seek an ironclad definition of Calvinism. I do not think it is possible to construct one. Rather, I prefer looking at Calvinism in terms of its existence as a living body of doctrines which, defying an absolute and definitive form, changes with predilections and circumstances to meet the needs of the different Reformed communities that embrace it.

As a living body of doctrines, Calvinism exhibits a great deal of development, diversity, and ambiguity. In fact, these qualities have been present within Reformed thought from its inception. Ulrich Zwingli himself—in many ways *the* father of the Reformed faith—developed views on subjects from the Lord's Supper to the nature of original sin that were discarded by the vast majority of subsequent Reformed theologians. Jonathan Edwards developed a position on the doctrine of justification that was, and still is, regarded by many as provocative, if not heterodox. Likewise, John MacLeod Campbell's view on the atonement has been criticized by many.

And this diversity continues. To look at the matter from a slightly different angle, consider B. B. Warfield—who was professor of theology at Princeton Seminary until 1921, an admirer of his predecessor Charles Hodge, and a theologian's theologian, who defended the doctrine of the verbal inspiration of the Bible against the rise of German rationalism and wrote on the church fathers and reformers and on themes like the doctrine of salvation and the errors of Roman Catholicism—and Jürgen Moltmann—currently professor emeritus of theology at the University of Tübingen, who was born five years after Warfield's death and whose works, such as *The Crucified God* and *Theology of Hope*, exhibit the influence of Hegel but rarely any interest in classical systematic-theological categories or in historical theology, and often take digressions to discuss themes such as feminism, anti-Semitism, ecology, the peace movement, and global political activism, often with little reference to either the Bible or church tradition. Both have a claim to the Reformed tradition. So do Rousas John Rushdoony, Greg Bahnsen, and Christian Reconstructionism; so do Tim Keller and the Redeemer Presbyterian Church in New York City; so do Hyung-Nong Park and Kim Jacjoon and both their sets of followers in Korea; so do the Reformed Churches in Hungary who are thriving following the political changes of the 1990s. All these perspectives claim the mantle of Calvinism.

So, diversity is present in abundance within the Reformed tradition. But how can such diversity be conveyed while still managing to treat the Reformed tradition in a coherent manner within a short introduction like this one? What I have decided to do here is to focus on themes that seem to me to be of enduring importance to the Reformed community and to attempt throughout the book to identify something of the range of opinions that have existed within Reformed thought on these themes.

The development of Calvinist thought appears in the writings of countless authors, a number of whom I list in the further reading section—writings which I have plundered for this good cause, and for which I thank the authors.

Jon Balserak
Bristol, England
17 June 2016

Acknowledgements

Gavin D'Costa, Paul Helm, Paul Balserak, Justin Stratis, Luke Perera, David Leech, and Isaac Chenchiah, made valuable comments on portions of this work. Andrea Keegan and Jenny Nugee proved expert editors and delightful people to work with. I owe much to an anonymous reviewer, who read an earlier version of this book. Useful suggestions were also made by so many people it is impossible to list them all. And as with everything, I am more indebted to my wife, Bilgay, than I can possibly say.

I dedicate this book to Ralph Keen. His enthusiasm for his students and for the service of others is truly inspirational, and his friendship and support are deeply appreciated.

List of illustrations

Chapter 1
Calvinism: what's in a name?

Calvinism is apparently newsworthy these days. A random sampling reveals: The *Wall Street Journal* from 23 October 2015 published an article on the Calvinist beliefs of the novelist, Marilynne Robinson. A piece in the 3 January 2014 *New York Times* hailed a 'Calvinist Revival' within US evangelicalism, and *Direction*, a Mennonite journal, printed an astonishing article in its Fall 2013 issue on, 'The Rise of New Calvinism among Canadian Mennonite Brethren' (Mennonites are traditionally strongly anti-Calvinistic). A *Guardian* article from 27 May 2009 bears the title, 'Chinese Calvinism Flourishes'. In the same month in 2009, *Time* magazine listed 'The New Calvinism' as one of the ten ideas changing the world right now. New Calvinism refers to a movement within conservative Christianity that embraces the beliefs of 16th-century Calvinism and holds that they are relevant to the 21st century. This obscure system of thought was placed on *Time*'s top-ten list alongside things like 'Biobanks', 'Ecological Intelligence', and 'Africa, Business Destination'.

This does not mean Calvinism is loved by all. To some, it is a dark, repressive force that has left a legacy of hatred and intolerance wherever it has gone. But be that as it may, this repressive ideology is currently making a comeback in both the East and the West.

Ulrich Zwingli, John Calvin, and Heinrich Bullinger

Searching for the roots of Calvinism, we find one of them in Wildhaus, in what is now north-eastern Switzerland, where Ulrich (or Huldrych) Zwingli was born in 1484. Like many young people at that time, he was inspired by Renaissance Humanism, the study of classical antiquity which began in Italy and spread throughout most of Europe. Learning ancient Greek, Hebrew, and Latin, Zwingli read the Old and New Testaments in their original languages. He also devoured the writings of the church fathers, especially Augustine.

He was a priest in Glarus and Einsiedeln before taking up the position of *Leutpriestertum* (people's priest) at the Grossmünster Church in Zurich in 1519. There he began preaching and writing in an effort to reform the Christian church. In 1523 and again in 1525, he engaged in public debates over things like how to worship God correctly. Zwingli's leadership led to wide-ranging moral and theological changes in Zurich and throughout the region.

Unfortunately for Reformed Christianity, Zwingli's life was cut short. He died on the battlefield in 1531, being caught up as an army chaplain in a war prompted by political disagreements associated with the Reformation, which arose between Zurich and a group of cities that had aligned themselves against Zurich. His death was lauded by Roman Catholics and also Martin Luther (who posted his famous ninety-five theses in Wittenberg in 1517), while his honour and godliness were defended by others.

One of his defenders, Heinrich Bullinger, took over Zwingli's position as people's priest. Zwingli and Bullinger each played extremely significant roles in the burgeoning Protestant Reformation. Their theology was related to, but distinct from, that of Luther. In fact, these two growing movements—Reformed and Lutheran—developed a tense relationship, characterized by suspicion and antagonism.

As Bullinger was beginning his ministry in Zurich, John (or Jean) Calvin (Figure 1) was not far away. Born outside Paris in 1509, he spent the majority of his adult life in Geneva, approximately 300 kilometres (170 miles) to the south-west of Zurich. He arrived in Geneva in 1536 after being forced to flee France in November 1533 because of alleged links to 'Lutheranism', a catch-all term during this time for heresy. Passing through Geneva in July of 1536, he was urged to stay in the city by Guillaume Farel, a fellow

1. John Calvin (1509–1564) by an anonymous painter.

expatriate and preacher working for reform there. Calvin stayed and, apart from being expelled for a brief period (1538–41), remained in Geneva for the rest of his life.

Calvin established Geneva as a major centre for the Reformation, with compatriot Theodore Beza joining him in the city in 1558. Like Zurich, Geneva became a bridgehead for the expansion of the Reformed church. Calvin preached more than 200 times per year and lectured through nearly the entire Bible, as well as writing numerous theological works. His *Institutes of the Christian Religion* is an exceptionally clear treatment of the major doctrines of the Christian faith. He, Beza, and the other ministers in the city trained and sent out pastors and missionaries both to nearby countries like France and England and also far-flung places like Brazil.

Although Calvin did not know Ulrich Zwingli, Calvin and Bullinger developed a close friendship. Their work as well as the work of individuals like Martin Bucer, Johannes Oecolampadius, Leo Jud, Peter Martyr Vermigli, and Wolfgang Musculus contributed to the development of a set of theological doctrines that would come to be known as Reformed theology or, for historically complex and anomalous reasons, Calvinism.

The spread of Calvinism

Much of the content of Calvinism was from its inception, and still is today, in line with traditional, especially Western, Christianity (think of the Apostles or Nicene-Constantinopolitan Creed). One thing that distinguishes Calvinism from other expressions of the Christian faith is its adherence to many of the theological emphases of Aurelius Augustine (354–430), the North African bishop and theologian, who produced works such as *The City of God*, *The Confessions*, and *On Christian Doctrine*. Calvinists have traditionally believed the theological foundations laid during the patristic era (roughly 100 to 600) to be of unparalleled significance and Augustine to be the pre-eminent interpreter of Christian theology from that era. His stress on the greatness and incomprehensibility of God, the sinfulness of humankind, and the sovereignty of divine grace was eagerly embraced by the Reformed tradition.

As this revitalized Augustinianism grew and developed, it spread from Zurich and Geneva throughout Europe, into the New World, and eventually Africa, the Far East, and the southern hemisphere.

From Geneva, Calvinism spread into France. What developed in France in the 1530s, 1540s, and 1550s, with Calvin and Beza's help, were groups of reform-minded men and women who embraced their vision of the Christian religion. These men and women came to be called Huguenots (the origins of the term are unknown).

Reformed theology also spread into Germany, particularly the Palatinate. This was due, in large part, to the change of that region's political head in the second half of the 16th century. When the position passed in 1559 to Frederick III, the Palatinate became one of the major centres of Calvinism in Europe. At the University of Heidelberg, important Calvinist theologians like Caspar Olevianus, Zacharias Ursinus, Bartholomäus Keckermann, and Jerome Zanchi laboured to propagate Reformed theology throughout the region.

Universities also played a significant role in the development of Calvinism in central and eastern Europe. In Hungary, for instance, the Reformed community established a theological academy in Debrecen for the furthering of the faith (Figure 2), and eventually accepted Heinrich Bullinger's *Second Helvetic Confession of Faith* (1566). Calvinist communities in places like Poland, Hungary, and Romania have survived to the present day, though often experiencing persecution from political authorities.

A DEBRECZENI REF. FÖISKOLA Ö ÉPÜLETE 1803^{IK} ÉVBEN A LEBONTÁS ELÖTT.

2. Debrecen Reformed College (Debreceni Református Kollégium) founded in Hungary in 1538.

Calvinist ideas were brought to Scotland largely through the efforts of Calvin's friend John Knox, though the earlier work of men such as Patrick Hamilton and George Wishart would need to be considered in any careful study of its origins there. Reformed theology was given eloquent expression in the *Scots Confession* (1560) and adopted by the Covenanters. Scottish Presbyterianism spread widely throughout the country, despite the efforts of Mary Queen of Scots, who was Roman Catholic.

Calvinism also wielded powerful influence over England at this time. In the 1640s, the English parliament called for ministers to gather at Westminster in order to draft a new order for how the church in the country would be organized and run. The *Westminster Confession of Faith* (1647) would be the chosen summary of Christianity for many Reformed churches in the coming centuries. This period also saw the rise of Puritanism. Theologians like William Twisse, Jeremiah Burroughs, John Owen, Christopher Ness, Richard Sibbes, and others would help develop Reformed theology, which was enthusiastically revived in the 19th century by Calvinist preachers like Charles Spurgeon and J. C. Ryle.

Calvinism's transplanting in American soil was brought about through, among other things, the efforts of Puritans like Cotton and Increase Mather. It would flower in the 18th century in the writings and preaching of Jonathan Edwards, the 'New England theology', and the revivalism of the Great Awakening, a religious resurgence which occurred in the United States between about 1730 and 1750. Equally important to its continued significance was the later blossoming in the American South of the Presbyterianism of Robert Lewis Dabney, John Girardeau, James Henley Thornwell, Benjamin Morgan Palmer, and Thomas Peck, with their accent on the spirituality of the church which we look at in Chapter 4. Also significant is the founding of Princeton Theological Seminary through the important labours of men like Archibald Alexander, Charles Hodge, and B. B. Warfield. The appearance in the 20th century of serious Reformed philosophers like Alvin Plantinga and Nicholas Wolterstorff, and the recent rise of the New Calvinists in the 21st century, suggest the continued influence of Calvinism in American life and thought.

The growth of Dutch Calvinism brought theological controversy to the Netherlands. In the late 16th century, Jacob Arminius and his followers took issue with the prevailing interpretation of Calvinist doctrine. This aroused disputes, which were not brought to a head until after the death of Arminius in 1609. The controversy was resolved in the Synod of Dordt which met from 1618 to 1619. The published *Canons of Dordt* discuss the well-known Five Points of Calvinism, which would be adopted by numerous Calvinist groups from that time until today.

The Dutch were at the forefront of bringing Calvinism to Africa. Around 1652, the Dutch East India Company arrived at the Cape of Good Hope in South Africa. This would eventually lead to the spreading of Reformed churches throughout South Africa and also to Calvinist involvement in the establishment of apartheid in that country in 1948. Calvinism has also spread over the centuries to other parts of Africa including modern-day Ghana, Cameroon, Nigeria, Zimbabwe, Malawi, and Sudan.

Calvinism was an extremely significant part of Dutch life and thought during the subsequent centuries. Though its influence waned in the 19th century, it was given new life through the so-called Neo-Calvinism of the theologian and politician Abraham Kuyper, as well as his compatriots Herman Bavinck, Herman Dooyeweerd, G. C. Berkouwer, Herman Ridderbos, and others. This would, in turn, influence 20th-century American Calvinist thought through, among other things, the work on apologetics (the defence of the Christian faith) of Cornelius Van Til and the cultural critique offered by Francis Schaeffer whose study centre, L'Abri, was founded in the Swiss Alps in 1955.

During the modern era, the birth of the dialectical theology of Emil Brunner and Karl Barth, also known as Neo-orthodoxy, has produced new strains of Calvinism. Neo-orthodoxy has been severely condemned by some Calvinists, who view it as a retrograde version of Christianity that accepts too many modernist assumptions about the unreliability of religiously oriented truth—a fact which leaves the legacy of Barth and Brunner on shaky ground in some quarters.

The growth and spread of Korean Presbyterianism through the work of Scottish missionaries in the late 19th century has made it one of the strongholds for the Reformed faith today. Here Hyung-Nong Park and Kim Jaejoon are of special importance. Park was the founder of a conservative form of Korean Calvinism, with strong emphasis on the traditional doctrines of the *Westminster Confession*. Meanwhile Kim developed Korean Presbyterian in more progressive directions, taking up ideas associated with dialectical theology.

Calvinism has also spread to South America, though its presence in countries like Brazil, Argentina, and Chile is dwarfed by the Roman Catholic Church. Much of its presence within South America is due to Scottish and Dutch missionaries, though Calvinism has established a foothold among the indigenous populations of countries like Peru.

Impact, enemies, Achilles heel

Calvinism's influence spans a diverse range of fields: theology, economic thought, art, politics, etc. This is part of what explains its impact. Calvinism attempts to deal rigorously with a host of profoundly important questions. What is truth and how do we come to know it? What is God? What is the purpose of life? How should we understand and organize human society? In addressing these questions, Calvinism has developed into a philosophy or a 'life-system', as Abraham Kuyper said.

Calvinism's impact has not always been salubrious. It has been provocative and socially disruptive. It makes claims which many consider outlandish and offensive. It asserts, for instance, that God wills everything that comes to pass, including horrific events such as the murder of six million Jews by the Nazis. It claims this while also asserting that God is absolutely just and holy. So, in other words, it insists that God can will sinful actions without being tarnished or stained. These assertions are hard for many to stomach.

This is perhaps one of the reasons individuals like H. L. Mencken, the American journalist and social critic, have lambasted Calvinism. 'What lay at the bottom of their savagery,' Mencken said of some of his opponents, 'was their idiotic belief in Calvinism—beyond question the most brutal and barbaric theology ever subscribed to by mortal man, whether in or out of the African bush.' Nor by any means is he the only one. Matthew Arnold, the Victorian poet and author of *Culture and Anarchy*, also despised Calvinism, as have many others.

Calvinists usually face their adversaries squarely, and are not known for gentleness. In fact, the Reformed tradition has, as Richard Mouw concedes in his thoughtful *Calvinism in the Las Vegas Airport*, often failed to deal as winsomely as it could with the outside world. The same is true internally as well. The Reformed have a history of splitting and squabbling with one another. As the late historian Albert Freundt self-deprecatingly joked: 'you don't have to be a Calvinist to be mean, but it helps'. The reasons that explain this dour disposition are complex, though Calvinism's adversaries enjoy suggesting otherwise.

Chapter 2
Conversion

One Sunday in 1642, John Owen—a man who would eventually become one of the most important Puritan theologians to ever live—went with his cousin to hear the famous Edmund Calamy preach at Aldermanbury Chapel in London. Arriving at the church, they were informed that someone else would be preaching in Calamy's place. The text his replacement (whose name we do not know) chose that morning was Matthew 8:26, 'Why are you fearful, O you of little faith?' By the time this stand-in preacher had finished his sermon, Owen had experienced a conversion. His doubts about God's love for him had vanished. As Owen's biographer, Peter Toon, observes: 'This spiritual experience cannot really be over-rated for it gave Owen the inward conviction that he was a true child of God, chosen in Christ before the foundation of the world, that God loved him and had a loving purpose for him.'

What is conversion?

Although someone might 'convert' from being a Conservative supporter to joining the Labour Party or from eating meat to being a vegetarian, the word is quite often used for describing religious changes. A person might convert, say, from Catholicism to Judaism.

Reformed theology, however, uses the term in a slightly different way. It still refers fundamentally to a change, but according to this way, everyone is born *un*converted. That is, they are born sinners; enemies of God; hell-bound. We might wonder how, according to Calvinism, the human race got itself into such a predicament. We will explore this in detail in Chapter 7, but suffice it to say for now, the answer has to do with the fall of Adam and Eve, which has left the human heart greedy, corrupt, and opposed to God.

So, can a person simply convert at will in order to be rid of this terrible problem? Yes and no. Actually in many ways, just no. Calvinism asserts two things about every person. First, people do not want to convert. They don't want to leave their sins. They love sinning. And, second, it is impossible for a person, by herself, to change this. Calvinism teaches that God is the only one who can convert a person. Conversion is a radical, inward change and God is its author. To be converted involves the renewing of a person's heart so that they love Jesus Christ and put their trust in him. This is what happened to John Owen.

There's more, too. Calvinists teach that God has already chosen those whom he will convert, selecting them before time began. This is the well-known doctrine of predestination which is so often associated with Calvinism. These chosen people, referred to as 'the elect', are the only ones whom God will convert. The rest, sometimes identified as 'the reprobate', God leaves unconverted and, thus, bound to suffer eternally in hell.

We might feel a sense of shock at this point. But let's not throw in the towel on Calvinism just yet. Its understanding of conversion exhibits sophistication and (believe it or not) compassion, despite its initially unwelcoming appearance. In order to see this, we might consider how it deals with several fundamental problems faced by most religious traditions seeking the conversion of other people, but problems that pose particular difficulties for the Reformed faith, for reasons we have just outlined. How to speak to someone about God's love. How to tell when true conversion has taken place. And how to address depression and human inability in relation to conversion.

Alarm to the unconverted

What would a Calvinist minister or theologian say to someone who, let us suppose, attended church some Sundays but had not become a member of any church and who felt unsure about what she believed? Such an individual fits comfortably within the experience of many people who have come into contact with Calvinist teachings over the past 500 years. Though it may be less applicable to the average reader of this book in the 21st century, it still does not seem so completely removed from their current circumstances as to be incomprehensible.

For starters, a Reformed minister would say to all the unconverted that conversion is a matter of the utmost importance. He would urge people to turn from their sins to God. Any idea that belief in predestination breeds a fatalistic attitude ('qué será será; what will be will be') runs completely counter to Calvinism's history. In the 17th century, English Puritans whom John Owen would have known, such as Richard Baxter and Joseph Alleine, wrote books with titles like, *A Call to the Unconverted* and *An Alarm to Unconverted Sinners*. The message they set out can still be heard today in the sermons of Calvinist preachers like J. Ligon Duncan III, the minister of the First Presbyterian Church of Jackson, Mississippi, Benjamin van Rensburg, the pastor of the Union Church in Istanbul, Turkey, and Nam-Joon Kim, the pastor of Yullin Presbyterian Church of Seoul, South Korea.

The Calvinist would also assure the unconverted person of the intellectual integrity of the Christian religion. Recently, for instance, Calvinists such as Paul Helm, a retired philosopher at

King's College, London, and Tim Keller, the pastor of Redeemer Presbyterian Church in New York City, have sought to offer such help. The latter's 2009 book, *The Reason for God: Belief in an Age of Skepticism*, is illustrative of this.

Speaking about God's love

But would a Calvinist minister tell someone who was unconverted that God loves her? Many would assume that *all* ministers would happily say this; that this was the single most important message a minister of the gospel could bring. But, for Calvinism, the truth of the matter is more complex.

While plenty of Calvinists today would be happy to tell a non-Christian (i.e. an unconverted person) that God loves them, traditionally Calvinists have been quite coy about this. This is *not* to say that they would not urge everyone to come to God, as we have already said. They would insist upon this intensely. But they would *not* necessarily feel comfortable saying, 'God loves you'.

If that seems odd, consider: love is ordinarily linked with intent. If God loves someone, then we may feel fairly justified in assuming that God intends to do them good. In Calvinist thinking, doing them good would seem to mean converting them and ultimately bringing them to heaven. *Could* God love someone but choose, for reasons undisclosed to us, not to convert them? Absolutely! God's wisdom is greater than human reason. Nonetheless, the fact that God's love can accomplish freely and without hindrance anything it wishes (as the majority of Calvinists believe) adds enormous complexity to the idea of speaking about that love and applying it to people.

Considering this complexity further, it might dawn on us that there is a line of thought a Calvinist *could* follow that might simplify matters. If God has chosen his elect and if he plans to convert them and bring them to heaven, then surely—the Calvinist might reason—God will only communicate with *the elect*. God will declare his love for them, make his intentions known to them, and ignore the rest of the human race. This would seem to make sense and to take away some of the complexity associated with speaking of God's love.

This line of thought is, however, not followed by the vast majority of Calvinists, who derisively refer to it as Hyper-Calvinism (some call it, High Calvinism) and consider it to differ from what the Bible teaches. The man most often labelled a Hyper-Calvinist is probably John Gill, an 18th-century English Baptist, but the label tends to be one that no one willingly owns.

To explore where most Calvinists fall on this question, I am going to broaden it slightly. The question's usual form, when discussed by theologians, is: can the gospel be offered to everyone indiscriminately? By 'gospel', we have in mind the good news of the salvation accomplished by Jesus Christ. This question is more general but still forces us to address whether God loves all people and whether God wants everyone to be converted and saved. After all, two biblical passages associated with the gospel message appear to say precisely this. John 3:16 declares: 'For God so loved the world, that he gave his only begotten Son'. Also 1 Timothy 2:4 states: 'God wants all people to be saved'.

One position on this question adopted by some Reformed theologians understands the gospel not as an *offer* but as a *command*. The position was strongly advocated by the British theologian, Andrew Fuller, who founded the Baptist Missionary Society in 1792, and is also associated with the English Reformed Baptist, Arthur Pink, who died on the Isle of Lewis in 1952. It does not offer God's love indiscriminately. In fact, it explicitly states that God does not love the reprobate, but only his elect. It insists, however, that the gospel's function is not to offer God's love but to convey an injunction. It declares that Jesus Christ died for sinners and that everyone is a sinner. The command, then, is: place your trust in Jesus Christ. Those who obey (who are God's elect, whom God himself converts) are saved.

A second position exists that does, in fact, understand the gospel as an offer of God's love and mercy made freely to everyone. It handles the problem of offering this to the non-elect by arguing that God has different aims for making his offer depending on the identities of his different hearers. In explaining this, Robert Lewis Dabney, the southern Presbyterian theologian and Confederate army chaplain during the American Civil War, contends that God has three aims in offering his gospel. The first is God's aim to save the elect. According to it, when a minister preaches the gospel, God also produces what theologians term an 'effectual call', which involves the powerful work of the Holy Spirit in the hearts of the elect. This enables them (who are scattered among the audience) to respond sincerely to God's love, accepting his gospel and becoming Christians. God's second aim in offering his gospel is to express his benevolence to all people, both elect and non-elect. This aim is *not* accompanied by an effectual call, for reasons which are known only to God. And God's third aim is to bring honour and glory to himself when his gospel offer is made to the reprobate and they reject it.

Opponents of Calvinism have criticized this position, particularly its proposing of God's third aim. Critics say it results in God making an insincere offer of his gospel to the reprobate whom God plainly and undeniably knows will never accept it. Answering this complaint, Dabney points to biblical passages that demonstrate God doing this. Compare, for instance, Exodus 5:1 with 7:3, 4. In the one text God says to Pharaoh, 'Let my people go', while in the other, God informs Moses, 'Pharaoh will not listen to you, in order that I may lay my hand upon Egypt'. The complaint is therefore nullified, Dabney contends, by biblical precedent.

We may assume, then, that theologians like Dabney approve of telling an unconverted person that God loves them, though these theologians still seek to ensure this declaration is not misunderstood. The word, 'love', can, of course, refer to a variety of different sentiments. As we have seen, Dabney is willing to speak about God's general love for all people, usually using the word 'benevolence'. But Dabney and others seek to ensure that God's *electing love* is reserved for the elect alone. In line with this, they usually interpret biblical texts like John 3:16 ('For God so loved the world') in such a way that 'the world' refers specifically and only to 'the elect'.

There's also a third position. In fact, some Calvinists are happy to switch between the second and third positions, to combine them, or even to allude, at different times, to all three of these views.

Theologians who espouse this third view find a division in the Bible's discussion of God's will. The Bible, they contend, discusses God's will as his *secret* decision (referred to by theologians as God's 'will of *decree*') to elect some people to salvation and also as his *revealed* will (God's 'will of *precept*') applicable to everyone. (We will discuss this division in more detail in Chapter 3.) The difference between them concerns the issue of whether God's will is effected or not. So, if God decrees something, it will *certainly* happen. If, however, God issues a precept, it might not happen; the precept embodies what we might refer to as a simple wish or desire.

The way this division applies to communicating God's love can be seen if we consider John Calvin's preaching. He contends that God needs to explain his will to people in this twofold manner because people are so mentally lethargic and slow to understand divine truth, and that it is important to understand this as one begins preaching the gospel. Calvin's approach to offering the gospel may be summarized as follows. First, no one knows who God has predestined (his will of decree). We simply do not have access to that information. Second, what we do know is that the Bible contains within it a general offer or call (his will of precept) to 'the world' (John 3:16) and 'all' (Matthew 11:28). Third, this general call does not provide a window into the breadth of God's saving will, for if it did then everyone would be converted and saved. Right now, this general call is all that God has revealed to us about his will. This means that Calvin places a biblical text like 2 Peter 3:9 ('God is not willing that any should perish but that all should come to repentance') under point two. This text does not convey to us the breadth of God's will of decree as it relates to salvation.

Therefore, God's general call is what should be proclaimed in all gospel preaching. It is intended for everyone, including the unconverted. So, Calvin issued a general call when he preached. Those who came to Geneva to hear him preach were a diverse collection of people which would have included Genevan citizens, refugees from various parts of Europe, and pleasure seekers who had come to hear the famous John Calvin preach. Surely, some unconverted people would have been in attendance. Calvin compelled them to claim the message of God's love as a message spoken to them personally, as this rather long quotation indicates:

> So likewise, when it is said in the scriptures that this is a true and undoubted saying, that God has sent his only begotten son to save all miserable sinners...every one of us must apply this particularly to himself, whenever, that is, we hear this general sentence, that God is merciful. Have we heard this? Then we may boldly call upon him, and even say: although I am a miserable and forlorn creature, yet since it is said that God is merciful to those who have offended him, I will run to him and to his mercy, beseeching him that he will make me to feel it. And since it is said, that God so loved the world that he spared not his only begotten son, but delivered him up to death for us, it is right that I should look to that. For it is very necessary that Jesus Christ should pluck me from that condemnation in which I presently am, since it is true that the love and goodness of God is declared unto the world in that his son Jesus Christ has suffered death. I must appropriate this to myself,

such that I may know that it is to me that God has spoken; he
desires that I should take possession of such a grace, and rejoice in
it within myself.

This comes from a sermon on Psalm 119. But Calvin also
frequently affirmed, when preaching, the reality of God's electing
love. When, for instance, Calvin preached on 1 Timothy 2:4 ('God
desires all men to be saved'), he insisted quite vigorously that this
text does not convey the extent of God's intention to convert and
save people. If it did, then every human being would be saved.
But, he noted, we know that God saves all sorts of people—Jew
and gentile, rich and poor, men and women, young and old—and
that a general call is made to them all. Thus, once again, we find
within Reformed thinking a concern to safeguard the integrity of
God's electing love which tends to govern the way the Reformed
speak about God's love.

In our fourth and final position, this concern is largely removed.
This view is associated with Amyraldianism, which is a form of
Calvinism that arose closely after Calvin's death (in 1564). The
name comes from Moïse Amyraut, who taught at the Academy of
Saumur in western France in the 17th century, though the position
was taught by others before him. It is sometimes identified by the
name 'hypothetical universalism'.

Whereas the positions discussed earlier have tended to privilege
the idea that God has chosen his elect and focuses his efforts on
bringing them to salvation, this fourth position sets aside this
concern in one extremely important way. It enthusiastically offers
the gospel and love of God to everyone without hesitation on the
grounds that Jesus Christ died for everyone; hence accomplishing,
at least hypothetically, the salvation of everyone. The idea that
Jesus died for everyone is denied by most Calvinists (who teach
that Jesus died only for the elect). Amyraldianism teaches,
however, that although Jesus died for all, God foresaw that not all
would accept his offer of salvation. Therefore, God chose to elect

some whom he would call and convert. Because of the approach it takes on several theological issues, adherents to this position claim it liberates them to speak boldly and without hesitation about God's love and about biblical passages such as John 3:16 and 1 Timothy 2:4.

A brilliant example of hypothetical universalism put into practice can be seen in John Preston's *The Breast-plate of Faith and Love*. Preston (1587–1628) was an Anglican cleric. In this collection of sermons, he probes and questions his hearers as to their willingness to accept God's gift of salvation won for them by the death of Jesus Christ ('Christ is dead for you', he famously declared). In these sermons, Preston is able to focus on his hearer's response, since the extent of Christ's death is not in question.

True and false conversion

With the gospel offer being made to an unconverted person, her response to it needs now to be considered. Convinced of the crucial importance of predestination, some Reformed theologians have encouraged a response that begins with introspection. The thinking here is that a person is supposed to search inside herself for signs revealing that she is one of those whom God has predestined—signs like sorrow for sin, a willingness to stop sinning, and a desire for forgiveness. Only after she has discovered these signs within herself is she permitted to believe that God's offer of salvation has really been made to her. But if she does not see such signs, she should *not* believe the gospel message to be offered to her.

This practice is referred to as preparationism, though preparationism is a term that can also be employed to refer to the idea that people can, or even *need* to, do certain things before placing their trust in Jesus Christ; things such as reading the Bible, attending worship, listening to sermons, and praying. These varying meanings obviously share the common idea that something precedes a person's full accepting of Jesus and his gospel.

Controversy over preparationism has taken different forms and arisen at different times in church history, perhaps most famously in the Marrow Controversy, which occurred in 18th-century Scotland. Against preparationism, many Calvinists have urged the freeness of the gospel message. That is to say, they have insisted that no 'preparation' is ever necessary or even possible. There is nothing a person can do to prepare themselves for God's love and mercy, which must simply be accepted as free gifts.

Now, to accept these gifts is to be converted. That is to say, anyone who truly accepts these gifts is only able to do so because her heart has been renewed by God. If this happens, as John Owen claimed happened to him, then she is no longer *un*converted but converted.

So, is it that easy? After all, anyone could *claim* to have accepted the gifts of God's love and mercy. Shouldn't we expect some proof? Such questions are taken very seriously by Calvinists. This being so, Reformed theologians have developed sophisticated ways of assessing the experience of conversion, developing them both to aid the convert and also to address the vexed issue of false faith.

False faith—which involves someone either faking conversion, perhaps to conform with the cultural norms of their day, or really thinking they have become a Christian but, in reality, have not—is believed by Calvinists to be relatively common. Reformed theologians point to many passages in the New Testament, such as Acts 8 (the story of the false faith of Simon the sorcerer).

In order to distinguish between true and false conversion, some Calvinists have produced schemes or 'morphologies of conversion', which identify the stages through which the soul moves in its journey towards conversion. Quite often six stages were set out, though the number varied. These steps ordinarily began with a person coming to realize their sinfulness and walked them through a deeply psychological journey ending in their coming to faith in the gospel, like this:

1. The sinner feels extreme worry and agitation which leads to a deep sense of concern over his condition.

2. The sinner turns to good works in an attempt to find a remedy for his anxiety. This fails, leading to even deeper despair and an intense awareness of his own sinfulness.

3. Feeling despair and misery, the sinner comes to understand all his attempts to rectify his situation are completely worthless in the eyes of a perfect God.

4. Now, the sinner begins to understand God's grace and develops an appreciation for it.

5. Gratitude and love for God indicate the presence of saving faith in the sinner, who is moved to live in thankful obedience and to be wary of the temptation to backslide again into sin and self-reliance.

This was adapted from something written by the Yale professor, Harry Stout, as a summary of the preaching of the American Puritan, Thomas Allen. We can see what Allen and other Puritans were trying to do, namely, setting out the path of true conversion. This served several purposes. It allowed anyone to identify whether they were on that path, or not. It was also pastorally helpful for the new convert, assisting her in making sense of what was happening to her. This enabled her to negotiate the experience of conversion intelligently. But schemes like Allen's morphology were also helpful for another reason.

They were used, particularly among the American colonies, as part of the process of becoming a church member. A person who was coming to request church membership would need both to confess her faith and also to narrate her experience of conversion. She would do this at a meeting in front of the leaders of the church. To confess one's faith ordinarily involves declaring *what* you believe. But to narrate one's experience of conversion could involve, depending on the ministers in attendance, a detailed explanation of a much more intensely personal nature. A morphology like the one described earlier gave ministers a blueprint they could follow when listening to such a narration.

Calvinists have, however, not always taken this approach when seeking to discern between true and false conversion. Reformed theologians have sometimes opted for much lengthier discussions of the nature of the converted heart. What does it look like? What characterizes it? Two of the best-known examples of such discussions are Thomas Shepard's *The Parable of the Ten Virgins* and Matthew Mead's *The Almost Christian Discovered: Or, the False Professor Tried and Cast*. Works like these have been reprinted in the 20th century by publishing houses such as the Banner of Truth Trust and contributed significantly to the rise (in the United States) of the New Calvinists.

But is conversion really that confusing, we may wonder. Shepard's *Parable of the Ten Virgins* runs to a staggering 622 pages in the standard edition (reprinted numerous times, most recently by Soli Deo Gloria Publishers in 1990). Is such length really necessary? Calvinists answer in different ways, but most of them would point to the real possibility of someone being tricked by a false prophet, by Satan, or by their own sinful hearts into thinking they possess a faith that they really do *not* have.

Discussions like Shepard's and Mead's have, in fact, often been produced during times of religious revival—precisely because during these times so many are claiming to have been converted. There was, for instance, a religious revival known as the First Great Awakening which occurred in the eastern United States beginning in the 1730s (followed by a Second and a Third Great Awakening occurring in America in later centuries). It was spurred on by the sermons of the English Calvinist preacher,

George Whitefield, who came over from England to preach throughout the colonies. Other revivals occurred during the 18th century, and subsequent centuries too, as Calvinists and other Protestants began to adopt a mindset favourable to world evangelization. Calvinist Revivals occurred, for example, in 18th- and 19th-century Wales and Holland, in 20th-century Romania and Korea, and in 21st-century China, to name but a few.

During these revivals, it has ordinarily been the case that people have experienced intense emotional states, which can include a range of (sometimes bizarre) behaviours such as fainting, barking like a dog, singing, screaming, laughing, and suchlike. The intensity and peculiarity of these experiences are, not infrequently, taken by some to be signs of their authenticity and of the authenticity of people's conversions. Yet, during almost every revival, disputes have arisen about these experiences and about the genuineness of the conversions being claimed, with many arguing that such unusual behaviours provide no solid grounds for believing that conversion has taken place.

During the First Great Awakening, the American philosopher and theologian, Jonathan Edwards, wrote *A Treatise Concerning Religious Affections* to address this question. Published in 1746, it is probably the most important analysis produced by a Calvinist seeking to discern the true character of conversion and to distinguish it from false conversion. In it, Edwards discusses the nature of human affections (the word 'affections' denotes the human will together with the emotions, but it points to something much deeper than simple feelings like sadness or happiness). Edwards explains the nature of what he calls 'holy affections'. Only true converts, he argues, exhibit such holy affections, which are characterized by a love for God and for God's holiness, a deep awareness of personal sinfulness, and deep appreciation for the beauty of biblical truth. Thus, true conversion has nothing, or very little, to do with mere emotionalism, Edwards argues.

But all of this analysis, taken up and pursued with the best of intentions, has produced some unanticipated side-effects. The seriousness employed by Calvinists in their work of distinguishing between true and false conversion has led to problems related to cases of over-analysis.

Perhaps the biggest problem can be seen in the fact that within some Calvinist communities it is not hard, even today, to find individuals who go to church their entire lives but refrain from ever joining the church because they never overcome doubts that their faith is genuine (these doubts leave them feeling that it is inappropriate for them to join the church, since that would be presumptuous). These doubts can hamper a person for decades despite the encouragement of her friends, relatives, and even her own minister. This problem occurs, it would seem, because the individual has been conditioned to believe that real, genuine faith (i.e. true conversion) is such a rare thing that someone ordinary like themselves can never experience it—a belief which is the effect of the intense scrutinizing of differences between true and false faith.

Attempts to address such problems have included efforts to stop people from focusing on themselves and the character of their faith and, instead, to consider God's mercy. So, for instance, the 19th-century Scottish preacher from Dundee, Robert Murray M'Cheyne, sought earnestly to help those who doubt by encouraging them: 'For every one look you take at yourself, take ten looks at Christ.' Also, the 19th-century American Presbyterian, W. G. T. Shedd, preached a sermon entitled 'Self-scrutiny in God's presence' which brilliantly explores these issues.

Depression and human inability

But these doubts can persist, and develop into serious depression.

Of course, some might suggest doubts and depression are quite reasonable if people are being told that God has already secretly chosen his elect before any of us were born. Indeed, predestination would seem to create all sorts of problems and lead to terrible depictions of a merciless, capricious deity who cares for no one and treats people like pawns. The Western literary canon furnishes us with many such depictions. Consider, for example, the Scottish poet, Robert Burns, and his well-known poem, 'Holy Willie's Prayer', the first stanza of which laments:

> O Thou, that in the heavens does dwell,
> Wha, as it pleases best Thysel',
> Sends ane to heaven an' ten to hell,
> A' for Thy glory,
> And no for ony guid or ill
> They've done before Thee!

One might also think of the work of another Scot, James Hogg. His gothic novel, *The Private Memoirs and Confessions of a Justified Sinner*, shocked 19th-century readers with its dark critique of predestination found in this tale about the two sons of Rabina Colwan and the murder of the older (George) possibly by the younger (Robert), who was a Calvinist. Scots are, of course, not the only ones who set forth such fearful images of a Calvinist world view. The American author, Herman Melville, broods over a cold, predestining God in *Moby Dick*. Similar reflections have arisen wherever Calvinism has gone.

These depictions have met with various responses by Calvinists. But the underlying concern fuelling them has been taken extremely seriously and dealt with quite carefully by Reformed theologians. That concern relates, ultimately, to the question of God's love and its availability to an individual person. This really is in many ways the key human question. Am I alone in the universe? Does the maker of the universe know I exist? Does he care for me?

Treating these fears has become a kind of specialty of Reformed theology. William Perkins, for instance, wrote, *The Whole Treatise*

of the Cases of Conscience: Distinguished into Three Books.
Likewise, Richard Baxter produced an enormous volume entitled
A Christian Directory, which is an encyclopaedic collection of
treatments for all sorts of mental and spiritual ailments, many
of which relate to these doubts and fears. Other Calvinists
have written books with titles like *A Lifting up of the Downcast*
and *Spiritual Depression: Its Causes and Cures*—the latter
being an extremely popular series of sermons by the Welsh
doctor-turned-preacher, D. Martyn Lloyd-Jones, delivered in
the mid-20th century.

So how do Calvinists address such depression? We can find an
example of the overcoming of it in the life of John Bunyan, the
English Puritan and author of *The Pilgrim's Progress.* In Bunyan's
autobiography, *Grace Abounding to the Chief of Sinners,* he
describes his own conversion, which involved a long bout of
depression, or melancholia as it was sometimes called.

Bunyan's anxieties began soon after his first forays into a serious
consideration of Christianity. He feared he was not one of God's
elect. He feared that God may have given up on him, leaving him
to his sinful lifestyle. He worried that he should not pray to God,
since someone in his condition could not pray without sinning.

Bunyan was temporarily relieved of these fears but eventually
plunged into a deep depression, because he suspected that he may
have committed the unpardonable sin. This is the sin spoken
about by Jesus in the Gospel of Matthew, chapter 12: 'Therefore
I say to you, any sin and blasphemy shall be forgiven people, but
blasphemy against the Spirit shall not be forgiven.' He eventually
overcame all this, through intense and constant prayer, which
has made his life story a valuable one to many wrestling with
similar issues.

But what makes Bunyan's analysis even more helpful is his
remarkable candour as well as his familiarity with his inmost

thoughts. He provides us with a window into a soul bearing the weight of depression. He sets out dates and times: 'I could not be delivered nor brought to peace again until well-nigh two years and a half were completely finished.' He bemoans his own condition: 'Now was I as one bound; I felt myself shut up into the judgement to come.' And throughout, he provides an almost clinical record of his soul's movements and feelings, and ultimately its recovery:

> I found two things within me at which I did sometimes marvel, especially considering what a blind, ignorant, sordid, and ungodly wretch but just before I was. The one was a very great softness and tenderness of heart, which caused me to fall under the conviction of what...[the Bible]...asserted; and the other was a great bending in my mind to a continual meditating on it and on all other good things which at any time I heard or read of.

His example has served as guidance for many.

But here the complaint might come: pointing a person to Bunyan does no good. Even *if* a Calvinist minister tells some unconverted soul to come to God and assures her that God invites her to come, and that she should look to someone like Bunyan as her example, the truth of the matter is that this unconverted soul *cannot* come to God. She is, as we said at the beginning of the chapter, *totally* dependent on God's converting grace. Without it, she will never be converted and never come to God. So (the objector may add) she may as well simply resign herself to await the outcome of God's sadistic game.

In response, the Calvinist minister cannot deny that this is precisely the gospel message he carries: place your trust in God, though you are totally dependent on God to do so. Given this apparent paradox, what does the Reformed minister do now? According to Robert Lewis Dabney, he does the following.

First, the minister insists that it is solely the fault of the unconverted person herself that she is not converted. In staying away from God, she (for reasons we will explore in Chapter 7) is simply following her own preference. Second, he asserts, or at least believes, that it is actually good for the unconverted to know of her inability. This knowledge functions to humble her before God. Third, while the temptation might be to send the unconverted to various means to assuage her sense of frustration over her own inability, Dabney encourages the minister not to take this route. Such means, he argues, are either likely to delude the unconverted individual into placing her trust in these means or, if she is perceptive, to prompt her to see that such means can do nothing to alter her condition and could involve her in sinning.

So, fourth, the minister simply reiterates to her the message of the gospel: 'believe in the Lord Jesus Christ and you will be saved' (Acts 16:31; see also Romans 10:13 and Matthew 11:28–30). If the unconverted person complains that she *cannot* believe, the unfortunate answer Calvinism gives her is: 'that is because you do not *want* to. So, how can you complain? You are merely doing what you (secretly) actually desire.'

If at this point the unconverted individual begins to feel her utter and total helplessness before God, Reformed theology would say the gospel is beginning to have its proper effect. And, the Calvinist minister might add, there is no safer place than to be knowingly and consciously at God's mercy.

But we have now mentioned the issue of consciousness which has been with us, usually under the surface, throughout this entire chapter. Here I mean specifically the idea of someone being conscious of her relationship to God, of the reality of God and her helplessness before him, of the question of God's love for her, of her deeply sinful heart, and so forth. In addition to being explicitly raised in the last paragraph, it was also raised in the story about John Owen with which we began the chapter. Owen became conscious the day he went to hear Edmund Calamy preach that God loved him and had made himself Owen's God. Conversion involves this, too. It is a renewing of the heart that produces—sometimes after a long, arduous struggle—a real and conscious peace with God and a sense of the reality of God that fundamentally changes everything for the convert. Much of what follows explores the character of this change.

Chapter 3
Culture

In 1913, a performance of Igor Stravinsky's 'The Rite of Spring' is reported to have caused a riot. Performed in the Théâtre des Champs-Élysées in Paris, this was the debut of the ballet choreographed by the innovative Russian dancer, Vaslav Nijinsky. The music itself is characterized by dissonant chords and a pulsating rhythm. Some reports recount elegantly dressed women throwing vegetables at the orchestra and even stabbing the person sitting next to them with a fountain pen.

Does such an event represent a display of culture or the dismantling of it? What *is* culture and how ought it to be understood? Philip Rieff, the American sociologist and University of Pennsylvania professor, argued that culture depends on the 'circumscription of sheer possibility'; that is, the very idea of culture depends upon imposing a 'pattern of moral demands' upon a society. Based on Rieff's thinking, this 1913 riot would seem to represent an attempt to destroy culture. Though someone might counter by saying that the riot represents an (admittedly over-eager) example of self-expression; freedom; the ability to act without constraints. After all, who wants to live in a society that tries to restrict the things we do? Surely (this objector might propose) the true nature of culture ought to be found in something other than the circumscription of sheer possibility—after all, possibility is not a *bad* thing.

What says the Calvinist? Before we answer, we might ask: is any of this actually relevant to Calvinism? Maybe not. Maybe Calvinists should disengage entirely from society. The idea is not as bizarre as it might sound. The Bible declares that 'the world' is evil (John 17:25; James 4:4; 1 John 5:19). It counsels: 'Do not love the world, nor the things that are in the world' (1 John 2:15). Christians are called to 'come out from among unbelievers, and separate yourselves from them' (2 Corinthians 6:17). The world with its pleasures is fleeting, Christianity teaches. 'The kingdom of God is within you', Jesus said (Luke 17:21). Therefore, the idea of disengagement from society—and, hence, from the questions we are asking about culture—may appear extreme but could, nonetheless, be what the Bible prescribes.

But in the judgement of many Calvinists, culture is profoundly important. As H. Richard Niebuhr said in his classic study on the relation of Christ and culture, the Reformed tradition has a more dynamic sense of the Christian's responsibilities in the world than do other traditions. This dynamism is associated with Reformed theology generally but perhaps especially with Dutch Neo-Calvinists like Abraham Kuyper, Herman Bavinck, Klaas Schilder, and more recently Herman Dooyeweerd, Henry Van Til, Cornelius Plantinga, and Richard Mouw.

God is king

We begin thinking about culture by considering God's kingship or will. Calvinism has found it helpful here, as has Lutheranism and other traditions, to speak of that will in two different and quite distinct ways. The first concerns speaking about what theologians refer to as God's 'will of decree' or 'decretal will'—the idea that God, before he created the universe, decreed (or willed) absolutely everything that has happened and is going to happen throughout human history. If a frog jumped from a rock into the Thames at 2.13 a.m. on 22 July 2013, God (Calvinism says) decreed that frog to do so. The second concerns speaking about God's 'will of precept'—the idea that God instructs people through precepts aimed at regulating human thought and behaviour. Through these precepts (think for instance of the Ten Commandments), he asserts his authority over all things—an authority that he declares to the world and wants everyone to acknowledge through their obedience.

Clearly according to the first of these, God is in total control. So, the Bible states: 'All the inhabitants of the earth are accounted as nothing. God does according to his will in the host of heaven and among the inhabitants of earth; and no one can hold back his hand' (Daniel 4:35). But according to the second, God's government would appear to be in tatters. People continually disobey him, refusing to acknowledge even God's existence. Calvinists contend that scripture testifies to this too: 'the LORD saw how great the wickedness of the human race on the earth had become, and that every intent of the thoughts of the human heart was only evil continually. And the LORD was sorry he had made human beings on the earth' (Genesis 6:5–6).

Calvinism teaches that these two conceptions of God's rule, though beyond human capacity to comprehend fully, nicely crystallize what the scriptures teach about God's will. They are not, Reformed theology contends, in conflict with one another but, rather, represent two perspectives which are helpful when considering various themes related to God's relationship with his creation.

How do they help? Calvinists believe they help by, for instance, clarifying the character of the mission of Jesus Christ. They reveal that Jesus was not sent in a desperate attempt by God to rectify a catastrophe he did not foresee. The mess we see today is not, Calvinism teaches, due to God having made a mistake or lost control. Rather, everything is under God's control. God created, God willed the fall of Adam and all the problems the world is currently experiencing, and God willed to send his Son to save the world. His purposes here will be accomplished just as his purposes have been accomplished up to this point in history. Nothing, Calvinism teaches, can thwart God's plan (i.e. his decretal will).

Now, what is that plan? To address this, we will introduce briefly the two-kingdoms doctrine (sometimes called the common-kingdom model), which we will speak more about in Chapter 4. Calvinists distinguish between God's governing of the world and his governing of the church. World and church represent two kingdoms or realms.

Some Calvinists maintain that God works redemptively in the church but not in the world; that the church is the locus of God's redeeming activity; that he has decreed to redeem her alone. Others believe that, while God's governing of the two realms are rightly distinguished, he is actually planning to redeem the whole creation; world and church.

To elaborate, our first group of Calvinists say that God is seeking to build his church towards the ultimate aim (decretal will) of bringing her to heaven to be with him. Meanwhile, that church is called (will of precept) to live in the world as 'strangers and aliens' (1 Peter 2:11) and not to look for God to change the world. Christ, as Michael Horton has argued, rules his church by his 'Word and Spirit' and he rules the world by his providence and common grace (something we will look at in a moment). The church's calling in this world is to declare the gospel, bringing people from the world into the church (Matthew 28:16–20).

Our second group, who are Neo-Calvinists, while not discarding the work of evangelism, believe that God has redemptive plans (decretal) which involve church and world. After all, do we not read: 'God did not send his son into the world to condemn the world, but that through him the world might be saved' (John 3:17)? These Calvinists believe this passage (along with others) teaches that God's plan is for Jesus to restore the whole of his fallen creation: human culture, society, and enterprise such that it will eventually be declared: 'the kingdom of this world has become the kingdom of our God and his Christ' (Revelation 11:15). Christians are called (will of precept) to 'bring every thought captive to Jesus Christ' (2 Corinthians 10:5) in every sphere of life. This understanding has been aptly described by Albert Wolters as 'creation regained'.

So, to be clear, both groups affirm God's lordship over every sphere of life, but their thoughts diverge on God's plans for these spheres and particularly on whether the cultural sphere is a part of his redemptive plans. To see how these positions affect their engagement with that culture, we need to unpack Calvinist understandings of culture.

The idea of culture and common grace

For Calvinists, culture does *not* refer merely to high culture, like the Stravinsky ballet referred to earlier. Nor is it pop culture. It might help if we consider that the word 'culture' comes from the Latin, *colere*, meaning to cultivate. So, we think of words like agriculture and horticulture. Yet, of course, human beings cultivate more than the ground. They cultivate a myriad of different things, from families to societies to traditions, within various arenas of life. In one very real sense, this is all culture. But more needs to be said. Calvinists do not conceive of culture as morally neutral. Thus, as cultures develop, they bear the marks of the moral dispositions of those who invest themselves in these cultures.

This raises at least two questions that will help us explore Calvinist understandings of culture more deeply. The first is, how can it be that cultures are as sane, sensible, and wholesome as they are? Calvinists do, after all, believe that the people who populate every culture are sinful. So how is it that they do not utterly corrupt these cultures?

35

According to Reformed theology, God restrains the sin of the world's cultures through something called 'common grace', which God exercises over all cultures. People naturally hate God and will continue to do so. This is the root problem within every society. But God's common grace fights against this influence by restraining sin.

What is common grace? It is his blessing upon all creation, life, and culture. This grace serves as a bedrock for the very idea of culture. Calvinists teach that without God's common grace, people would have destroyed the world already. Common grace does not bring about a person's conversion (which is the work of God's special grace), but is God's universal blessing that brings general goods to a society: justice, common decency, courtesy, and kindness. The idea of common grace acknowledges human sinfulness while also insisting that all things, even human sin, are under the control of God. Thus, through God's common grace sin's power and influence are restrained.

Common grace is common to both believer and unbeliever alike. 'God causes his rain to fall on the just and the unjust' (Matthew 5:45). One of its most important expressions is in the human conscience. People, despite the effects of the fall, still know right from wrong; they still feel the pang of conscience when they steal something from a shop or tell a lie. This is an incomparable blessing, and the result of God's grace operating in the world.

Calvinism teaches that because of common grace, many who make no pretence of being Christians have appeared throughout history doing remarkably altruistic deeds. The Calvinist would be quick to qualify this point by explaining that these good acts are actually not good in the eyes of God. They are, after all, performed out of a heart that hates God (which is the condition of every unbeliever's heart). Yet, they are good according to human judgement and essential for the thriving of a healthy culture.

Common grace differs in its expressions from one society to another. Where the rule of law has been set in place and is followed, a society will invariably be more salubrious. In another place, if cultural breakdown has occurred, it may not be safe to walk on the streets even during the daytime, let alone at night. Common grace can also exercise greater or lesser influence over a given culture—a fact which theologians point to in order to help explain the moral decline that visits regions and countries at different times in their history.

The second question that the moral character of culture raises is this one: is just everything culture—more specifically, can such a thing as *bad* culture exist? On this question, Henry Van Til (writing in the 1950s) argued that culture can be godless or godly. The character of a culture depends on the spirit that animates it. People engage in such an extraordinarily wide variety of cultural pursuits: educational, scientific, exploratory, artistic, and so forth. And while the Calvinist (Van Til would insist) pursues all of these endeavours with the desire of pleasing God, the fact is that others who are less inclined towards Christianity will work in the opposite direction. But it is all culture.

Other Calvinists have taken a rather different approach, and I think a more perceptive and useful one, particularly given the moral state of the Western world at present. Here, we can return to the thinking of Philip Rieff. Though not a Calvinist himself, his understanding of culture has been influential and is alluded to not infrequently by Reformed thinkers like, for instance, Carl Trueman of Westminster Theological Seminary.

Like Rieff, Trueman thinks of culture as defined by what a society forbids. He aligns culture with 'the elaborate structures and materials built into the very fabric of society for the refinement and transmission of its beliefs and its forms of life from generation to generation, connecting past, present, and future'. Thus, not everything is culture. Culture must bear a particular kind of moral stamp if it is to be rightly called culture. The *laissez-faire* permission to do anything is immoral and, hence, not rightly called culture.

On this basis, Trueman contends that in the West, and America particularly, we are not merely witnessing a move away from Christian culture but rather the rise of 'anti-culture'. America, Trueman contends, has lost anything that can legitimately be called 'culture'. He has, on this basis, encouraged Christians to come to terms with the fact that the culture war has been lost and that the church ought to begin to consider whether the language of exile is not perhaps appropriate for describing her current condition. The church lives (Trueman and others too suggest) in exile in a strange land; the image comes from the Old Testament and from Israel's being taken into exile in Babylon.

This does not, he is quick to say, mean Christians should disengage from society and go off and live in a cave. Trueman, who would not self-identify as a Neo-Calvinist, is, rather, saying that they should understand the situation in which they live. They should not have any illusions about it. In particular, he offers a gentle criticism of those Christian individuals and groups who pine for a lost age and take every opportunity to remind the world that their nation used to be a Christian one. He urges deeper reflection on the best ways to engage with society.

Calvinism and the cultural mandate

What does all of this mean for the Christian's interactions with culture? How does the Calvinist seek to obey God (will of precept) in light of his understanding of God's plan? We will speak more about this in Chapter 4, but one thing to say here is that the assumption might be that the Neo-Calvinist would be more upbeat than Trueman and might urge robust and confident engagement with culture whereas Trueman and other Calvinists would encourage disengagement, apathy, and perhaps even antipathy. But, as I have just said, that is not true. The reality is more complex.

It is true that the differing views held by Calvinists concerning God's plans for the two kingdoms influence understandings of what cultural engagement means. But the fact is, all Calvinists take seriously the calling they have from God to serve him in every aspect of their lives, including cultural engagement. Calvinists do not support or encourage separation from culture; they would in fact openly criticize such thinking. But those who do not believe God plans to redeem culture would tend to view their cultural engagement more from the perspective of the benefit it can offer to the church.

One practical way that all of the Reformed interact with culture can be seen in the idea of callings or vocations. The basic idea here is that Calvinists propose thinking about human life in terms of spheres or arenas. Each has its own particular responsibilities, logic, and rhythm. Home and family. Work and leisure. Friendship and commerce. Whatever circumstances someone finds themselves in, those circumstances represent the callings God has given to them and offer them opportunities for spiritual service through which they may pursue their cultural mandate.

It would be wrong to think, the Calvinist contends, that a woman cannot serve God if she is a lawyer, homemaker, graphic designer, or accountant; that she must be a nun or minister of the gospel to have a calling to serve God. According to Calvinism, she ought to think of her position (whatever that position is) as a Christian calling. As a Christian, she is to obey God wholeheartedly within every situation she finds herself. 'Only, as the Lord has assigned to each one, as God has called each, in this manner let him walk' (1 Corinthians 7:17–18).

This view of life, Calvinists contend, infuses the most banal portions of everyday existence with meaning. Spiritual service is not to be especially sought in a monastery or in some lonely place in the desert. It is to be sought everywhere. Life is replete with encounters through which the Christian has the privilege of pleasing her God and influencing the culture in which she lives, says Calvinism.

It is true, we should add here, that Neo-Calvinism in particular embraces (what is sometimes called) a transformational agenda: cultural expressions should be brought into alignment with what Jesus desires for them. This pursuit of what Henry Van Til called 'world conquest', takes different forms. Some of the particular arenas within which it might be pursued, such as the political, will be looked at in greater detail in Chapter 4.

Calvinism's cultural legacy

Fuelled by this understanding of God's kingship, of culture, of common grace, and of the duty to serve God in all spheres of life, Calvinists have laboured and left their mark upon the world.

The basic idea of the Christian community spreading to other portions of the globe and seeking to plant God's kingdom in these places can be seen well before the rise of Neo-Calvinism. Among the Massachusetts Bay colony and John Winthrop's notion of being the 'City on the Hill', living conscientiously for the glory of God, this group of Christians exhibited brilliantly the Calvinist idea that God has dominion over the world he created.

In the 17th century, Calvinism was a driving force behind the expansion of knowledge and, in particular, the study of human nature. This led to a critical reframing of a host of questions associated with the limits of human knowledge. This, in turn, served to promote the pursuit of ways of knowing and to drive an experimental programme which contributed to the development of the empirical sciences. Involved in the pushing forward of this programme were Calvinists, such as the 19th-century scientist,

James Clerk Maxwell, who formulated the classical theory of electromagnetic radiation. Maxwell's belief, and that of some of his contemporaries, was that his work as a scientist was fundamentally driven by his belief in God; that one can make sense of the universe precisely because an intelligent being had designed it.

Moreover, Calvinists introduced into the West a new way of conceiving of time, as Max Engammare, director of the Librairie Droz and research fellow at Université de Genève, has recently argued in *On Time, Punctuality, and Discipline in Early Modern Calvinism*. Roman Catholics during the Middle Ages and Reformation era had conceived of time as primarily cyclical, following the liturgical calendar of the Catholic Church with its seasonal rhythms that repeat each year. European Calvinists—who dispensed with the liturgical calendar and still today do not celebrate Christmas and Easter as religious holidays (though they may participate in them as cultural festivals)—introduced during the 16th and 17th centuries a view of time that was linear and finite. With this came an appreciation of time as precious. People learned to be on time for appointments, which had previously not been a concern.

Work on the arts by H. R. Rookmaaker, a Dutch philosopher and art critic, provides another example of Calvinist influence. Rookmaaker worked to understand art. His thinking can be found in works such as *Modern Art and the Death of Culture*. By the mid-1960s, he was invited to start the Department of Art History at the Free University of Amsterdam, attracting a large number of foreign students to the department at a time when this was still far from typical. Rookmaaker influenced another individual, Francis Schaeffer. Schaeffer, a Reformed philosopher and apologist, eventually started a study centre in Switzerland called L'Abri. At this centre, which opened branches in different parts of Europe and the United States, many students came to research Christianity and its relationship to culture during the turbulent decades of the 1960s and 1970s. Schaeffer would go on to have a marked influence on several generations during the 20th century. He also contributed to thinking on the environment with his book, *Pollution and the Death of Man*, published in 1970.

This Calvinist mandate to order the world has also produced less desirable results. The example regularly pointed to is the case of the Afrikaner Calvinism that developed following the establishing of an outpost of the Dutch East Indies Company at the Cape of Good Hope in 1652. Although refugees came from various parts of Europe (France, Belgium, England, Scotland, etc.) to South Africa, the Dutch Reformed Church took root in the country and required effective allegiance to itself by those arriving in the country. As Calvinist theology developed within South Africa and adapted to deal with the idea of the covenant community dwelling among the 'heathen' indigenous population, it came eventually to see that population—even those black South Africans who had converted to Christianity—as demarcated by racial difference. With this difference becoming deeply accepted within the white Christian community, the idea of seeking to establish the authority of Jesus within South Africa took on a political aspect which led to not only the establishing of white minority rule within the country but also the implementing of measures designed to keep God's people pure in the faith. This pursuit of purification and protection led to the policy of population control known as apartheid.

Interestingly, Allan Boesak, one of the leading black figures fighting against apartheid, was also a Calvinist. He employed a Neo-Calvinist conception of culture in his fight, arguing that apartheid actually contradicted the very Calvinist ideal that Afrikaner Neo-Calvinists ought to be pursuing, namely, the global authority and sovereignty of God. So, Abraham Kuyper famously declared that 'not a square inch of human existence' is free from the reign of Jesus Christ. If that is so, then God's reign among blacks in the country is as indisputable as his reign among whites.

Adding to these examples, we might note that Calvinism has, for good or ill, been one of the forces that bequeathed to modernity conceptions of human sinfulness, predestination, and dour seriousness towards everyday life which have saturated Western thought. The presence of these ideas can be seen in literature, for instance—thinking of individuals such as the Scottish poet, Robert Burns, or of earlier poets like the Puritan, Anne Bradstreet, or more recent authors, like Emily Dickinson, T. S. Eliot, John Updike, or Marilynne Robinson. Themes of depression, sin, and conversion appear in Nathaniel Hawthorne's *The Scarlet Letter* as well as Edith Wharton's *Ethan Frome*. Updike's *In the Beauty of the Lilies* explores Clarence Wilmot's loss of faith, interpreting it in terms of the absence of divine grace which Calvinism contends is essential for true belief. Even films like *Apocalypse Now* and *No Country for Old Men* have been pointed to as evidencing the influence of Calvinism in their depictions of the darkness of the human heart.

Liberty, capitalism, and the Protestant work ethic

Many would include the idea of liberty among these powerful Calvinist notions that have so profoundly affected the modern world. They would add, too, the work ethic that some say is the driving force behind free-market capitalism. And, to be sure, Reformed thinking on these powerful notions was important to their development, though other traditions also played their parts.

The links between Calvinism and these ideals grew over time, with the French philosopher, Voltaire, the American author, Harriet Beecher Stowe, a sprawling collection of historians, theologians, and other academics, and even several prime ministers and presidents all contributing to this growth. It was, of course, Voltaire who remarked that Calvinism fights 'for the liberty of the people'.

The association between Calvinism, hard work, and material prosperity rode this same wave, being reinforced by the role played by Protestant countries like Germany, Britain, and the United States in the industrial revolution of the 19th century. Indeed, many saw (and still see) a natural partnership between liberty and financial prosperity.

We cannot go further without mentioning Max Weber's well-known essay, *The Protestant Ethic and the Spirit of Capitalism*. What is intriguing about this book is that, once considered within its historical context (it was written in 1904 and published a year later), we can see that Weber, a German sociologist, had not come up with the idea of a link between Protestantism and capitalist profit-seeking out of a clear blue sky. Rather, he was echoing a belief that was commonly held at the time. What was novel about his thinking was the idea that this pursuit of profit was driven by a deep desire among Calvinists to demonstrate their divine election (i.e. the fact that they had been predestined by God).

Weber's analysis has been criticized but his work is still studied in-depth in sociology, politics, and economics. It has, in particular, been argued that any link between Calvinism, liberty, and capitalism almost certainly belongs solely to the 19th-century world out of which it came. Yet even critics of Weber's thesis have conceded that it has become a self-fulfilling prophecy, being believed by so many Protestants for the last one hundred years that it has taken on a life of its own.

Thus, whether Calvinism *was* responsible for the linkage between these ideas is irrelevant among many Presbyterians, Calvinistic Baptists, and other members of today's Reformed community. So true is this fact that the influence of Weber's *Protestant Ethic* is now growing stronger in Asia and South America today. In both places, the social and economic teachings of Kuyperian Neo-Calvinism are making inroads within the Reformed community, giving new life to ideas which John Calvin himself would almost certainly have been ignorant of and in which he would have likely had little interest.

Chapter 4
Church

Calvinists believe Adam and Eve were the first church, established by God following their fall into sin in the Garden of Eden. Since that beginning, God has always maintained his church, though it has been attacked relentlessly by the world and the devil and, at various points in history, reduced to small groups of believers, usually identified as the 'remnant'.

One such point in history was the 16th century. At that time, theologians like Ulrich Zwingli, Heinrich Bullinger, and Johannes Oecolampadius argued that the Catholic Church had been taken captive, metaphorically speaking. It was no longer governed by godly ministers but by a succession of popes all of whom were in league with the devil. Seeking to combat this, these reformers proclaimed defiantly that Jesus Christ must have sole authority over his church. They also claimed that they had been raised up by God to restore the church. These concerns ultimately led them to separate from the Roman Catholic Church (which they came to believe was no longer a church in any meaningful sense) and form new churches, which spread throughout Europe and beyond. Thus was born Calvinism or the Reformed faith.

Today, a number of church denominations align themselves with Calvinism: the Presbyterian church, Anglicanism, Congregationalism, some forms of Methodists and Baptists, and

denominations identifying themselves as 'Reformed', such as
the Christian Reformed Church or the Reformed Church in
Slovenia, or as 'Free', such as the Free Church of Scotland. All
of these denominations have local churches scattered around
their respective countries. So, for instance, someone who was in
Romania could attend a church service at a church belonging to
the Reformed Church in Romania (Biserica Reformată din
România). There is, to provide one example, such a church that
meets on Traian Street, Dej 405200, in that country.

Character and purpose of the church

Reformed thinking on the church, as with so many other topics,
begins with distinctions. Many Reformed theologians, for
instance, distinguish intellectually between the *visible* church,
that is the visible community of Christian believers on earth (i.e.
local church congregations) and the *invisible* church, that is the
invisible assembly of all the elect throughout history. Calvinism
teaches that God has selected, before he created the universe, a
group of people who would dwell in heaven with him for eternity
and others who would suffer in hell. The elect are the former
and they are the *invisible* church, some of whom are presently
on the earth, some who are already in heaven, and some who are
yet to be born. Though some theologians, like John Murray of
Westminster Theological Seminary in Philadelphia, have taken
issue with this distinction (specifically, the concept of the invisible
church), the majority of Calvinists have acknowledged it as valid
and useful.

Some Calvinists, specifically Abraham Kuyper and those who
follow him, also distinguish between the church as institution and
as organism. The former refers to things like the organizational
structure of the church, the form of discipline within it, and issues
related to the celebrating of the sacraments. The latter refers to
the idea that the church is a living organism. It grows organically,

having its centre in heaven. The church was, says Kuyper, an organism before it became an institution. The organic church also has an influence which expands into society, influencing and sanctifying culture.

Calvinists further delineate the character of the Christian church by identifying her as the mother of the faithful. Why, then, might someone attend church? Part of the answer is that the Christian *needs* to. The church is her mother and provides her with spiritual food in the same way that a child needs her earthly mother to provide bodily nourishment. Calvinists, then, do not regard the church as an optional part of Christian life. This is expressed more eloquently by ancient writers, like Cyprian (210–258), who declared: 'You cannot have God for your father if you do not have the Church for your mother.' This is articulated in the *Scots Confession* (written in 1560) which says 'outside of the kirk there is neither life, nor eternal felicity'.

Christians need their mother, Calvinism says, because without her they will not survive. Life is so hard and the spiritual temptations so great that someone attempting to face them without the support of a local church which they attend regularly will not be able to do it. He will fall away and stop following Jesus Christ. God has raised up his church in this world as an essential means of support for his children.

To explore this further, we need to say something about church membership. According to the Reformed tradition, it is essential for the believer that she be a member of a local church. The procedures for formally becoming a member vary considerably from place to place but ordinarily involve professing faith and taking an oath by which a person submits to the church. The belief is that, in doing so, he is submitting himself to Jesus Christ, who has appointed these leaders. If the Christian refuses to do this, then discipline cannot be practised.

Though the word 'discipline' may conjure up images of harsh treatment, it should not. Church discipline is intended to be an expression of love. It involves care, oversight, guidance, and encouragement. It may be expressed variously depending on culture, custom, and other factors. For instance, during his years at Kidderminster, the Puritan minister, Richard Baxter, visited all of the 800 families in his church every year, teaching and counselling them individually. Whatever form it takes, discipline is designed to express affection.

The practice of church discipline does not imply a belief that the church can be perfectly pure. Calvinists are Augustinian in their views on this issue. That is, they believe that the church will, while on earth, be a mixed body—it will always contain within it both true and false Christians (false Christians are those who do not truly believe). Calvinism teaches it is better to try to care for everyone than to try to weed out the true from the false right now—a process that awaits the final judgement.

This discipline applies to the family unit. Most Calvinists believe that infants of church members are themselves church members. It is for this reason that the Reformed community (except Reformed Baptists) practises infant baptism. Baptism is the seal of the covenant. 'The seals of the covenant', said Francis Turretin, the 17th-century Swiss-Italian Reformed theologian in his *Institutes of Elenctic Theology*, 'pertain to those to whom the covenant of God pertains. . . . [and] . . . the covenant pertains to infants.' Once baptized, the infant grows up in the church. She will, even from a young age, start learning some kind of Christian instruction, called a catechism (from the Greek word, κατηχισμός), employed within the Christian church from antiquity.

This discipline aims to bring the child to a personal faith in God. Once the child comes of age, at roughly eighteen years old, she would be expected publicly to declare her faith and formally to join the church. She is already a member by virtue of her baptism but now she must own that baptism.

But what is meant when we say infants of Christian parents are church members? Are they Christians? Much ink has been spilt on this complex issue. A scholar as respected as David F. Wright, for years Professor of Ecclesiastical History at New College (Edinburgh), argues that the *Westminster Confession*, for instance, teaches 'baptismal regeneration'. Others, such as Derek Thomas, disagree with Wright. *The Directory for Publick Worship* (which accompanies the *Westminster*) seems to side with Wright when it says of these infants: 'they are Christians, and federally holy before baptism, and therefore are they baptised'. But the *Westminster* adds statements like, 'the inward grace and virtue of baptism is not tied to the moment of the administration of baptism', which introduces the kind of qualifications that seem to support Derek Thomas.

Baptismal regeneration refers to the idea that baptism causes the recipient of it to be born again by the Holy Spirit. Apparently, the *Westminster* wants to distinguish the act of baptizing from the inward grace of God that causes someone to be born again but still wants to call the infant a 'Christian' even before he is baptized. The vast majority of Reformed thinkers today do not believe the *Westminster* teaches baptismal regeneration. The phrase 'they are Christians' was dropped from subsequent revisions of the *Directory*.

Returning to discipline, among Calvinists it has also traditionally involved the use of excommunication. Excommunication (despite the dreadfulness of the word) represents a kind of powerful medicine used for the Christian's good. If a believer is excommunicated that means that she is forbidden from taking part in the sacrament of the Lord's Supper. Once she has corrected her behaviour and convinced the church that she is ready to obey her Lord Jesus again, she is again allowed to participate in the

Lord's Supper. Excommunication is intended to be a kind of shock to the system—to awaken the sinning Christian to the seriousness of her sin, so that she will stop sinning. It is reserved for serious or ongoing sinful behaviour. It is a last resort, after discussion and admonition have failed. All these issues are discussed at length by Reformed theologians, with particularly insightful analysis being produced by a host of 19th-century thinkers such as James Bannerman, James Henley Thornwell, and Thomas Peck.

Finding the church

In the towns and cities of many countries around the world, there are numerous local churches to choose from. How does a Christian find one to attend?

To answer this, we might first note that the Reformed community has traditionally been persuaded that false churches abound. By 'false' they meant and sometimes still mean, primarily, the Roman Catholic Church. Calvinists, not to mention Lutherans and many other Christian groups, point to biblical passages (e.g. 'Watch out for false prophets. They come to you in sheep's clothing, but inwardly they are ferocious wolves', Matthew 7:15) to elucidate this belief about false churches. Calvinists have also traditionally believed that the Pope is 'the Anti-Christ, that man of sin, and son of perdition, that exalts himself, in the Church, against Christ and all that is called God', to quote the *Westminster Confession* again. The Anti-Christ is mentioned in the New Testament (1 John 4:2–3; 2 Thessalonians 2:3–4). What Calvinists mean is the papal office. Whoever holds the office of Pope is the Anti-Christ. A superb explanation of this belief can be found in volume three of the *Systematic Theology* of Charles Hodge, the American Presbyterian theologian and principal of Princeton Theological Seminary, who died in 1878.

Reformed theology teaches that because false churches abound, the Christian's search for a true church must be guided by the

Bible, which sets out two 'marks' identifying it. These are the true preaching of the gospel and the correct use of the sacraments. To these, they have sometimes added discipline (there's that word again) as a third mark. So we find in the *Belgic Confession* (1561) of Guido de Bres:

> The true church can be recognized if it has the following marks: the church engages in the pure preaching of the gospel; it makes use of the pure administration of the sacraments as Christ instituted them; it practices church discipline for correcting faults.

Thinking on these marks was hammered out during the 16th century in an environment discernibly different from today, but the idea has been rejuvenated recently by Mark Dever, pastor of Capitol Hill Baptist (in Washington, DC), who identifies nine marks of a healthy church: (1) preaching, (2) biblical theology, (3) the gospel, (4) conversion, (5) evangelism, (6) membership, (7) discipline, (8) discipleship, and (9) leadership. Dever's analysis offers a fresh and brilliant reading of the matter.

Looking at the traditional three, the true preaching of the gospel, the Christian message of salvation ('gospel' means 'good news'), refers to interpreting the Bible accurately and, principally, to describing the person and work of Jesus Christ correctly. Jesus must be depicted in the gospel as the Son of God and the one who takes away our sins. Being restored to good relations with God—an idea usually referred to as 'justification'—must be described as completely the work of God, so that God receives all praise and honour for it.

To use the sacraments correctly means, first, identifying that there are two: Baptism and the Lord's Supper. (By contrast, the Roman Catholic Church identifies seven sacraments.) It also means administering these two sacraments in a way that is pleasing to God.

As regards baptism, I have already mentioned that the majority of Calvinists believe baptizing infants is what God instructed his church to do. Other issues related to things like the method of baptizing, whether by dunking the person under water or merely sprinkling water on the forehead, are subjects over which differences are permitted.

As regards the Lord's Supper, Calvinists hold a number of different positions, but are all united against the Roman Catholic position, known as transubstantiation, which teaches that the bread and wine used in the Lord's Supper are actually changed, during the church service, into the body and blood of Jesus Christ. Calvinists eschew any idea that the bread and wine change. Instead, they usually teach that through the bread and wine believers are raised up spiritually to a deeper fellowship with Jesus Christ, who is in heaven. This is accomplished through the believer contemplating, by faith, that Jesus gave his body and shed his blood for her.

We have already spoken quite a lot about discipline, but one additional aspect of the Calvinist's celebrating of the Lord's Supper that nicely conveys how the Reformed practice discipline is something called 'fencing the table'. Calvinists believe (because of 1 Corinthians 11:17–34, which warns of taking the Supper in 'an unworthy manner') that it is wrong for a Christian to participate in the Lord's Supper if he is not spiritually prepared to do so. This being so, many Reformed church ministers see it as their duty to try to dissuade such individuals from participating. This work of discerning between those who are spiritually prepared and those who are not has sometimes, in some places, involved handing out 'communion tokens' to individuals. Before the celebrating of the Lord's Supper, the minister examines the members of his church. This involves asking about their spiritual life. Once he has done so and found the member is spiritually healthy, he gives them a token. Only those who have a token in their possession when they come to church are permitted to partake in the Supper (Figure 3).

3. Stock Communion Tokens dated 1843, Free Church of Scotland.

Jesus is King of the church

When the believer becomes a member of a church, he has
(Calvinism declares) submitted himself to Jesus Christ, who
governs that church through its ministers. If anyone tries to
command him to do something that violates God's commands, the
Reformed faith teaches that he must disobey the command.

The authority that has traditionally been most likely to issue
such a command is the civil government. The question of the
relationship of church authority and civil authority is, therefore,
one that has been explored extensively by Reformed theologians.

The question is a particularly vexed one both because the
development of societies has historically tended to have a religious
element associated with it (i.e. a common religion which
permeates that society and seems indistinguishable from it)
and also because the Christian Bible provides relatively little
clear-cut guidance on distinguishing intellectually between state
power and church power. Both are described in scripture as
gifts from God. This similarity may seem banal but is not, and
was rendered even more complex through the conversion
to Christianity of the Roman emperor, Constantine, in 312. He
went on to decriminalize Christianity, which swiftly became
the religion of the Roman Empire. From that time forward, the
fundamental question of whether civil or ecclesiastical authority

is ultimate became extremely fraught. And today the same conflict often rears its head.

Many Calvinists have claimed that these two powers and the authority they wield can be intellectually differentiated through something called the two-kingdoms doctrine (initially associated with Lutheranism); it has, more recently, been called the common-kingdom model. The idea is discussed by John Calvin, who explains that 'there is a twofold government in man'. One aspect is political (i.e. this-worldly), associated with the civic realm, our bodies, physical needs, etc. The other is spiritual, associated with God and 'the life of the soul'. Over each, he says, 'different kings and different laws have authority'. Continuing, Calvin says he will elaborate on 'civil government' and 'church laws' in different places in his *Institutes of the Christian Religion.*

Having distinguished these two realms, the Reformed have consistently argued that civil government ought not to intrude into church affairs nor should it seek to usurp authority over a person's conscience. It ought not to attempt to influence the teachings, decisions, and worship of the church. Likewise, Calvinists have insisted the church not meddle with the affairs of the state but, rather, confine itself to matters within its remit, that is, spiritual matters. This thinking developed, in the United States, into the notion of separation of church and state, which is now such a fundamental part of American life.

The boundaries of the church's remit are sometimes discussed under the umbrella phrase of the 'spirituality of the church', a subject which has received ample consideration within Reformed circles with some of the best work on it being done by 19th-century American Presbyterians like Robert Lewis Dabney, Charles Hodge, C. R. Vaughan, and William Boggs. The thought on the topic by one such Presbyterian, Stuart Robinson, can be seen in *The Church of God as an Essential Element of the Gospel, and the Idea, Structure, and Functions Thereof.* Published in 1858, it discusses the subject by beginning with the idea of the church and its intimate relationship to God's plan of salvation. Robinson goes on to demonstrate that if, in fact, God intended the church to be intimately linked with his plan to save his elect, then the church *must* be separate in its focus and purposes from the work of civil government.

The two-kingdoms doctrine has played an extremely important role within Calvinism, but it does raise difficult questions. One of them is what the church's remit looks like *in practice* vis-à-vis the state. What constitutes intrusion into the secular sphere? It has been easy enough for Reformed theologians to say that the church should not support a political candidate during an election, as that would be a clear intrusion into the secular sphere, but it has a harder time with more complex situations. What if, for instance, the civil government is actively involved in sinning? Should the Christian church say something? Should, for example, the Reformed church have spoken out against the practice of slavery, or the Nazis' treatment of the Jews, or the brutal Ceauşescu regime of the 1970s and 1980s?

Calvinists have often disagreed on how to answer this question, but some of the clearer thinkers on it today have insisted that the church not lose sight of what it means to have dominion over the spiritual realm. Michael Horton, for instance, has argued, 'there is nothing in the "two kingdoms" or "spirituality" doctrine to keep the church from declaring to the civil powers directly what it proclaims to the world from the pulpit'. That is, as it is the church's calling to denounce sin, it must denounce it wherever it finds it, including the state. This does *not* permit the church to tell the state how it ought to conduct its affairs but only to tell the state that it has violated God's law and must stop.

There are other questions that the two-kingdoms doctrine raises. In fact, the subject is being intensely debated today, with new subgroups and nuanced positions appearing almost daily:

2K (Two Kingdoms), R2K (Radical Two Kingdoms), NL2K (Natural Law Two Kingdoms), the common-kingdom model, Theonomists, Kuyperians, Neo-Kuyperians, Neo-Anabaptists, Neo-Reformed, etc. At present, the Reformed community welcomes dialogue on such important issues, but some are understandably concerned about the tendency for well-meaning thinkers to caricature opposing positions and about the harm this might cause. So, for instance, some have contended that many of the two-kingdom or common-kingdom understandings 'remove God from the public sphere', leaving the present life, food, clothing, home, job, family, and leisure as things about which God *does not care*. This, however, was clearly not Calvin's view and it is not the view of someone like Horton, David VanDrunen, or Darryl Hart. On the other side of the debate, the Neo-Calvinists, Kuyperians, or Neo-Kuyperians (all of which are sometimes called Transformationalists) are said to hold a position that blurs any distinction between the church and the world and downplays the impact of sin. This, likewise, is *not* a fair depiction of the position of someone like Albert Wolters or Richard Mouw.

State and church

The same set of issues continues to take centre stage as we consider the specific question of whether the civil authority should support the Christian religion. This, again, is a taxing question for Reformed theology and some of their answers may surprise us.

If we search the writings of John Calvin, for instance, we find that the primary duty of the ruler is to ensure the 'flourishing of the true religion'. In his assessment, the church and the civil government function as 'two eyes' directing the body in the right way to please God—the body being the Genevan commonwealth and, by extension, any commonwealth. He distinguished the spheres over which church and state had influence (as we just discussed), but saw both as having the same ultimate aim. A very similar position is set out in the initial version (1647) of *The Westminster Confession of Faith*, though chapter 23 'on civil magistrate' was rewritten in 1788 to reflect a much stronger belief in the separation of church and state.

The coordinating of these 'two eyes' can be witnessed in Geneva, where the civil government cooperated (albeit with plenty of disagreements over policy and practice) with the city's Christian ministers in enforcing Christian beliefs and practices within the city. Economic matters were influenced by Christian teaching, as were legal, cultural, and educational issues. Taverns were closed, though they were eventually reopened; most forms of dancing were forbidden. People were put to death for heresy, homosexuality, divorce, incest, witchcraft, and other offences. Such broad cooperation between church and state was, in fact, common in many European cities at the time—including, say, Zwingli's Zurich.

In the case of Geneva, two of the committees that liaised with the main civil governing body (the Little Council) were quasi-religious in character. One was the board of the procurators for the General Hospital, which was responsible for the care for the poor and widows, housing of orphans, the disabled, and other handicapped individuals. The other committee was the Consistory, an institution which spread to numerous Calvinist cities and towns throughout Europe, especially France. The Consistory, made up of members of Christian ministers and of the civil government, served as a morals court.

The Consistory met once a week (ordinarily) to hear cases that varied from instances of marital disharmony to economic injustices, witchcraft, gambling, dancing, slander, adultery, murder, heresy, and anything else that was deemed to have breached the morals appropriate to a Christian commonwealth. The Consistory worked in concert with the Little Council and would hand individuals over to the legal system if the offence warranted it, but it also administered admonitions, requirement to pay reparations, bans from the Lord's Supper (which were similar to what we described earlier in this chapter regarding excommunication), and excommunications (which were more serious, and involved exclusion from the church altogether and often banishment from the city). Moreover, if you were banned or excommunicated you could not marry and could not be guaranteed access to poor relief.

Those in Geneva who were put to death were executed by the city government (not the church). The fact that the government executed criminals, including those guilty of *spiritual* offences like heresy, exhibits the profound collusion apparent between church and civil government among the Reformed during this era. That collusion has now vanished from Western countries, as has the executing of heretics and numerous other categories of crime—but, at the time, these executions received a vigorous defence from Reformed theologians such as Calvin, his protégé, Theodore Beza, and many others.

As Reformed thinking developed over time a division gradually began to appear. Some forms of Calvinism continued the church–state cooperation seen in places like Geneva while other forms witnessed a lessening of collaboration and in some cases an increase in hostility. But here I am not referring to the kind of practical hostility that Calvin and Beza often experienced in Geneva (where the Little Council didn't want to implement their plans), but to a more fundamental hostility which has today become a part of some Calvinists' own outlook and has moved them to adopt an *in principle* opposition to church–state cooperation. Such philosophical opposition does not appear in Calvin or Beza or most of their contemporaries, but developed over time.

Now, the classic question that has been dealt with for centuries by theologians and other theorists when thinking about the civil government relates not so much to the issues of cooperation, but rather to the issue of how a Christian is to respond to the state when it becomes tyrannical. Should the believer resist passively? May she ever resist actively? Can she rise up in armed resistance against a tyrannical government? How is *any* form of resistance justified?

Tyranny itself is difficult to define, but ordinarily, as far as historical Reformed thinking is concerned, it involves some kind of command to sin and specifically to engage in idolatrous worship. The classic biblical passage, as regards Reformed theology's assessing of the matter, is probably Daniel 6, which describes how the prophet Daniel refused to obey the command to bow down and worship an idol.

In thinking through this question, early Calvinists ended up helping to develop thinking on the idea of the contract, or covenant, and its applications for political thought. The civil head, these Calvinists contended, holds his authority from God on the basis of a contract which has stipulations that he must obey. These stipulations varied within Reformed thinking, but were often focused on what they believed was the primary duty of the civil authority, which was (as we have seen) ensuring the flourishing of true religion. If the head of state fails in this duty, and particularly if he imposes idolatrous worship on his citizens, then he would be deemed to have broken the covenant. Calvinist theologians such as Samuel Rutherford, who wrote *Lex, Rex or The Law and the Prince*, were significant in the development of this thinking.

On the question of whether the individual Christian can rise up against his government, thinking has developed considerably within Reformed circles over the centuries. What we see is a gradual move from a refusal to identify any situation in which individuals are permitted actively to resist their government, to the contemplation of scenarios in which such resistance would be permitted. Some Reformed thinkers, from Calvin to Peter Martyr Vermigli, proposed the idea that members of a government have the right—in fact, the duty—to rise up to protect the people from a tyrannical king. But in later centuries, different scenarios were envisioned. If, after all, everyone in the chain of authority within a government is part of the problem and the situation is morally intolerable, then Reformed thinkers (and others) began to reckon that the ordinary people themselves must organize either to separate or to overthrow the existing authorities by the least forceful effective means. If that meant armed resistance, then such an action would be permitted. The solutions devised tended to represent developments of the so-called Just War Theory (which deals with the moral justification for why wars are fought) and also elements of Natural Law (which contends that certain moral truths are part of human nature and intelligible to everyone through human reason).

According to Reformed theology, none of this takes away from the fact that Christians may well be required to suffer persecution as Jesus Christ did. Nor, Reformed theologians argue, may Christians use revolution to avoid this. But, as already indicated, they may engage in revolution for certain reasons. It was, it seems likely, because of the careful work done on these issues by numerous Reformed theologians during the 16th and 17th centuries that Presbyterians were among the most zealous advocates for the American Revolution. They had, it would seem, a sophisticated ethical argument already within their tradition.

Worshipping the King of the church

When the believer becomes a member of a church, he also begins a life of worshipping God. While in many ways, the typical worship that occurs in a Reformed church does not differ enormously from what occurs in other church groups, there are a few things that can be mentioned as noteworthy.

Traditionally, Reformed churches have decided to plan what happens during Sunday morning worship by adhering to the 'regulative principle'. It states that the church should only do in worship what she is explicitly told to do in scripture. During the 16th century, this involved a marked simplifying of worship. The Roman Catholic worship practised throughout Europe at the time used candles, holy water, various rites and rituals, incense, chants, and other practices that reformers like Zwingli, Bullinger, and others set aside.

In the place of Roman Catholic practices, these Calvinists put a simpler liturgy that involved preaching, singing, praying, and the celebrating of the two sacraments of Baptism and the Lord's Supper. These sacraments were only celebrated intermittently, not every Sunday. The frequency with which the Lord's Supper was, and still is, celebrated varies enormously from one Reformed church to another.

The Reformed also changed the style of preaching. Calvinist preachers decided to choose a particular book of the Bible and then to preach from the beginning to the end of that book without skipping anything. What this involved was a careful explaining of each paragraph—and sometimes each sentence and, to some extent, even each word—of a biblical book. This style, referred to as continual reading (Latin: *lectio continua*) produced long series of sermons. John Calvin, for instance, preached 200 sermons on the Old Testament book of Deuteronomy. Jeremiah Burroughs, the English Puritan, preached forty-one sermons on The Beatitudes (twelve verses, found in Matthew 5:1–12). Later Calvinists did not always follow this same pattern, as can be seen by glancing at the sermons of Charles Spurgeon, the great Calvinistic Baptist preacher, who was called to pastor New Park Street Pulpit (in London) at the age of nineteen, only four years after his conversion (Figure 4).

Many Calvinists during the Reformation believed they should sing the biblical text during worship. They believed, and some still believe, this is the only thing one should sing in worship. The

4. Charles Spurgeon preaching at the Metropolitan Tabernacle.

portion of the Bible they sang was the book of Psalms. The Psalms are, after all, poems that were sung by the Old Testament people of God. They loved, and still do love, the idea of singing God's Word back to him. Accordingly, 'exclusive psalmody', as this is usually called, is still practised by some Calvinist churches throughout the world.

The particular day that this worship is to be performed has traditionally been Sunday; a day referred to by some Calvinists as the Christian Sabbath. This word (Sabbath) appears, of course, in the Ten Commandments. Calvinists argue that the day was changed, by Jesus, from Saturday which is the Jewish Sabbath, to Sunday. They argue this on the grounds that Jesus, following his resurrection on the first day of the week, began a pattern of meeting with his followers on that day. This was, and is still, interpreted by Calvinists as a sign that Jesus wanted the day to change, so that the Christian community learned to celebrate the day on which the Lord Jesus rose from the dead. The 'keeping of the Sabbath' has, among some Reformed communities, taken on very specific guidelines and prohibitions. The idea has developed that Sunday is (what the Puritans used to call) the 'market day for the soul'. It is on this day that the Christian rests from all worldly business and focuses on the health of her soul. Accordingly, many Reformed churches will have a morning church service and later an evening service on Sundays, so that the whole day can be devoted to spiritual nourishment.

The Sabbath day ultimately represents, Reformed theology teaches, the final rest God's church will find in heaven. The church, then, is God's appointed means to ensure that his elect are brought to enter this rest in heaven. God's Son, Jesus, is appointed as head over it, and in this capacity Jesus accomplishes the work given to him by his Father.

Chapter 5
Knowledge

The character of what, according to the Reformed tradition, can be known about God is captured beautifully in these words from Job 26:14: 'Lo, these things are but the fringes of his ways'—words which the Puritan, Stephen Charnock, took for his lemmata in the tenth discourse of his *On the Existence and Attributes of God*. This image of the fringes, parts, or edges of a garment nicely captures Reformed understandings of all theological knowledge. It is firm and sure knowledge, but extremely limited.

While much of this limitation is due to the inscrutable nature of God's being, it also flows from the fact that God is a person. Theological knowledge, according to Calvinism, is knowledge of a person and as is true with all persons, if God does not reveal what is on his mind, we will never know it. We can guess at it, just like someone can guess why their friend did not meet them at the theatre the way she was supposed to, but, at the end of the day, the real reason will remain mysterious until it is revealed. The same, according to Calvinism, is true of God; unless he reveals his mind, people will not know it. The corollary is also true, namely, that gaps will invariably exist in human knowledge about God when God chooses to remain silent about something.

A further limitation to this knowledge about God is, according to the Reformed faith, located in the human heart. Due to sin's effect on human thinking, people do not want to know the true God. Rather, people are, the Calvinist insists, continually trying to invent their own God and to reduce God to something manageable and fully comprehensible. This has the effect of contaminating or corrupting true theological knowledge.

One of the best examples of this God-reducing tendency is the human propensity to create counterfeit gods, or what are called idols. Reformed theologians have traditionally exhibited great concern over this, so intense among 16th-century Reformed Christians that it prompted outbreaks of iconoclasm. Iconoclasm is the act of smashing icons, statues, and anything that was deemed to represent an idol. In parts of Switzerland and Germany, the Netherlands, France, and elsewhere Calvinists rampaged through cities smashing statues, breaking them into pieces—a visceral reminder of the intensity of religious beliefs and the feelings they can provoke. To these men and women, anything—any image, be it a statue, sculpture, or painting—that was supposed to represent an image of the invisible God or of the saints to whom Roman Catholics offered veneration was so offensive that it should be obliterated (Figure 5). The same intense concern is shared, though thankfully without the accompanying physical destruction, by Reformed ministers and theologians today, as can be seen in books like Tim Keller's recently published *Counterfeit Gods*.

None of this bodes well for the possibility of theological knowledge. But Reformed theologians are not daunted. So, Herman Bavinck, the Professor of Theology at the Free University of Amsterdam who died in 1921, could declare that 'mystery', an attribute related principally to God's incomprehensibility, 'is the life-blood of dogmatics'.

What we should learn from this as we begin to examine Reformed conceptions of theological knowledge is *not* that this knowledge is fundamentally irrational in character but that it is of a particular

5. Calvinists destroying statues in Catholic Churches, 1566 (engraving).

kind. Reformed theologians dispute any charge of irrationality. It is not irrational, they point out, to believe things that cannot be fully comprehended. If it were, human beings would hold very few beliefs. What is irrational, they counter, is to refuse to believe something for which one has strong evidence—and it is the claim of Calvinism that the truths of Christianity are supported by strong evidence.

Not only is theological knowledge of a particular kind, but it also must be preceded by an internal change in the knower. Calvinists contend, in other words, that theological knowledge requires that the heart problem alluded to a moment ago be rectified. In other words, theological knowledge belongs to believers alone. 'We shall not say that, properly speaking, God is known where there is no religion or piety' in the knower, as Calvin said—we will clarify later in this chapter what this means.

Sources of theological knowledge

In order to know God, the right approach must be taken, which, for Calvinism, requires the drawing of distinctions. A basic distinction traditionally made by Calvinists is between God's own knowledge of himself and the knowledge humans can possess about him. The latter is referred to by various terms such as 'our theology' or the 'theology of pilgrims' (Calvinists, like many Christians, believe life on earth is a pilgrimage or journey towards heaven). Here the words 'our' and 'pilgrims' indicate the weakness of this knowledge, which is profoundly different from God's own self-knowledge. This weakness will, in part, be rectified once Christians arrive in God's presence in heaven, but their knowledge will never come even remotely close to the character of God's own knowing of himself. This distinction highlights the divide between God and humankind.

It is worth briefly mentioning before we proceed that the understanding of this distinction embraced by some theologians carries with it the idea of dissimilarity. This was, in the medieval and early modern eras, sometimes asserted in the form of a slogan: 'between the finite and the infinite there is no proportion' or 'no analogy'. The slogan can be found in some of John Calvin's sermons, for instance. Karl Barth puts it more eloquently: 'one cannot speak of God simply by speaking of man in a loud voice'.

Other portions of the Reformed tradition, however, would eschew such extreme thinking on dissimilarity. As a way of approaching the matter of human knowledge of God, the idea conveyed in this slogan arguably raises more questions than it answers. If there really is no analogy at all between human beings and God, then knowing God would seem to be impossible. What does it mean to call God loving, for example, if God is completely different from every man and woman who have ever lived? I suspect, therefore, that theologians, like Calvin, probably employed this slogan rhetorically to emphasize God's greatness and did not follow through consistently with all its implications. Nonetheless, the slogan and the problems it raises further highlight the difficulty of navigating between the Scylla of exalting the otherness of God and the Charybdis of worshipping a false god created by the human mind.

So, what, according to Reformed theology, are the sources of theological knowledge? Where does 'our theology' come from? The simple answer is that it comes from nature and from the Bible. These are the two places or two books, as they are sometimes called, where God has chosen to reveal himself. But both of these were subjected to devastating critiques during and after the European Enlightenment. Thus, before exploring more exhaustively the sources of 'our theology', we first need to look at how Calvinism has responded to these critiques.

During the Enlightenment, the Scottish philosopher David Hume and others savaged the idea of inferring anything from what we see in the world around us; thus attacking nature as a source for theological knowledge. Likewise, German scholars such as F. C. Baur and Julius Wellhausen began questioning the veracity of the Bible on historical and textual grounds. Their work of 'higher criticism' (as it came to be known) presented significant problems to the Reformed belief that scripture is an utterly trustworthy source for knowledge about God. Likewise, Albert Schweitzer (author of *The Quest of the Historical Jesus*) and others raised serious questions about the possibility of discovering, through the New Testament, Jesus as he really was. Immanuel Kant, the Prussian philosopher, raised important questions about what, if anything, can be known about God. Kant argued in books like *Critique of Pure Reason* that we do not have access to things in themselves (the so-called noumenal world) but our experience of things is always experience of the phenomenal world as communicated to us by our senses. Of course, if we are limited to sensory perception, this would seem to preclude the possibility of knowing anything about the spiritual realm, God, heaven, and hell, since these things are not accessible to our senses.

Calvinist responses to the Enlightenment have varied enormously. Karl Barth, the Swiss Reformed theologian who died in 1968, responded by accepting (albeit with some caveats) the findings of higher criticism and a Kantian understanding of knowledge but arguing that God could 'break through' to communicate to humankind in moments of 'crisis'. The 'theology of crisis' as this approach has been called is adhered to by other Reformed figures, such as Emil Brunner, T. F. Torrance, T. H. L. Parker, and Reinhold Niebuhr. The crisis of which they speak is one that is forced upon a person when she is confronted by the awesome antinomy between the created world and the transcendent God. This notion of antinomy or dialectic is at the heart of Barth's thought, leaving him in something of an interesting position with respect to our question about the sources of theological knowledge. He would seem to bypass that question, since he stresses God's free self-revelation which is not bound to the use of specific sources. As John Webster says, 'For Barth, God's Word is never available in a straightforward way. It is not a deposit of truth upon which the church can draw.'

Other Calvinists responded by discarding the conclusions of men like Hume and Kant and choosing instead to adopt philosophical positions devised by other Enlightenment luminaries. They adopted these positions and used them to defend the veracity and reliability of scripture and nature as sources of theological knowledge against Enlightenment attacks. For instance, American Calvinists like John Whitherspoon, Archibald Alexander, Charles Hodge, A. A. Hodge, Robert Lewis Dabney, and B. B. Warfield adopted (with varying degrees of fidelity) Scottish Common Sense Realism, which was the brainchild of Thomas Reid and Dugald Stewart. It enabled these Calvinists to assume the original powers of the human mind to form valid judgements about reality on the basis of data presented by the senses and, thus, to oppose the prevailing scepticism and rationalism of their day. Such opposition may be surveyed in Dabney's *The Sensualistic Philosophy of the Nineteenth Century*, which critiques thinkers like George Berkeley, Thomas Hobbes, John Locke, John Stuart Mill, and Herbert Spencer.

Other Calvinists, such as the Dutch-born Cornelius Van Til, chose to discard Enlightenment findings but to attempt to move beyond men like Hodge and Warfield. Van Til, who was influenced by Warfield and also by Abraham Kuyper and other Dutch thinkers, briefly taught at Princeton Theological Seminary before joining the newly formed Westminster Theological Seminary. He sought to develop a distinctively Reformed approach to the questions of knowledge and the defence of the Christian faith. His thought is complex and subject to various interpretations. It insists on the utter reliability of the Bible and denies the notion of neutrality. Because human beings have been profoundly affected in mind and heart by the fall of Adam, it is ludicrous (he contends) to speak about a kind of neutral arena as regards human knowing. No one, Van Til said, looks on the Christian Bible or the natural world (the two sources of theological knowledge) as an objective observer. Rather, everyone approaches them with a collection of presuppositions which they are committed to and according to which they judge all things. For the Christian and the non-Christian, Van Til insists, these are fundamentally different.

As regards the specific matter of criticism of the Bible, Reformed theologians like Robert Haldane, James Bannerman, James Orr, J. Gresham Machen, Ned Stonehouse, and E. J. Young defended the scriptures by, among other things, developing sophisticated understandings of the character of divine inspiration. These understandings sought to come to terms more thoroughly with the human authorship of the Bible while also asserting its divine inspiration; that is, that the Bible ought to be viewed as God's own

Word. Here B. B. Warfield's *The Inspiration and Authority of the Bible* is a classic.

Turning again to the content of the 'two books', Reformed theology elaborates on the knowledge people glean from these books by distinguishing between natural and supernatural theology.

Natural theology

Nature theology is theological truth derived by observing nature; i.e. the world and universe. The world and entire universe are believed by most Calvinists to reveal truths about the God who made them. An additional element of this natural revelation concerns an inner or innate knowledge present within all of people regarding God's existence. It is called by John Calvin a 'sense of divinity', by Francis Turretin 'the testimony of conscience', and by Charles Hodge 'innate' and 'intuitive' knowledge.

To support the legitimacy of natural theology, Calvinists usually point to biblical passages like Psalm 19, in which we read that the heavens declare the glory of God. They also point to Romans 1:19–20, which explains that 'through the things that are made' people understand aspects of God's attributes, his wisdom, power, and goodness. Regarding the idea of an innate sense of divinity, Calvinists point to Romans 2:15, which speaks of the law of God being written in every person's heart. They also note that throughout numerous centuries of human existence, people have borne witness to a belief in God or gods.

Though many concur with this reading and with the legitimacy of natural revelation, some demur, including Karl Barth, G. C. Berkouwer, and Gordon H. Clark (Cornelius Van Til's understanding of natural revelation is disputed). The debate around these questions has continued into the late 20th and early

21st century, with many authors weighing in, including John Gerstner, R. C. Sproul, Vern Poythress, Greg Bahnsen, Norman Geisler, and John Frame.

Those who do believe in the legitimacy of natural revelation concede that it is non-saving; that is, it cannot bring about personal conversion. It cannot teach people about their sin. It teaches nothing about God's sending of his Son, Jesus, to die for humankind. It also, crucially, cannot remove sin from the human heart or mind (the results of Adam's fall). It is, however, most Reformed theologians would say, the source of non-Christian philosophies, such as the ideas of Plato and Aristotle and of other religions, such as Buddhism and Hinduism. It has also been useful through the centuries in discussions of ethics and politics.

Belief in the existence of natural revelation among Calvinists usually leads to the concomitant belief in the *non*-existence of atheists. In other words, many within the Reformed tradition would argue that everyone—even those who vehemently deny it—knows that God exists. They cannot *not* know this. If people deny God's existence, the truth is they are suppressing it in the way people suppress a memory too painful to recall. The knowledge people have of God is (so the argument goes) based on natural revelation, which cannot fail to communicate truth about God. This is limited knowledge, but it *is* knowledge.

In fact, Alvin Plantinga, a Notre Dame University professor of philosophy who recently retired, contends that belief in God is 'properly basic'. In other words, people can assume God's existence, taking it for granted in the same way they take the existence of other human beings and the existence of history for granted. No one asks for evidence that, for example, other people exist. They *assume* it, despite not having objectively verifiable proof (remembering, of course, that it could be that the people we see before us are figments of our imagination). So, people may also assume God's existence, says Plantinga, in writings such as his *Warrant and Proper Function*.

Supernatural theology

Supernatural theology ('our theology') is much fuller and more substantial than natural theology. Calvinism teaches that it includes not only the existence of God and his power, wisdom, and goodness, but also knowledge about Jesus, his life, death, and resurrection, his divinity and humanity, the creation and fall of the human race, and such like—essentially, the contents of (what is often summarized as) the law and the gospel.

Supernatural theology is the product of the three members of the Trinity. It will be recalled that for Christianity, and the Reformed tradition in particular, God exists in Trinity. That is to say, there is one God who exists in three persons, the Father, the Son, and the Holy Spirit. All three are involved in the creation of this knowledge.

Calvinism teaches that God, in order to overcome the impotency of natural revelation, revealed himself in his Son, Jesus Christ, from whom 'our theology' comes. Jesus is the Eternal Word of God. 'In the beginning was the Word. The Word was with God and the Word was God' (John 1:1). Jesus, the Son, because he has dwelled eternally with the Father and the Holy Spirit is able perfectly to reveal God to the world. Therefore, just as Calvinists identify Jesus as King (as we saw in the last chapter), they also identify him as Prophet.

Calvinism teaches that this revelation is now found in sacred scripture, which is the product of the Holy Spirit's inspiration. In the scriptures Jesus reveals not simply the will of God considered generally but he reveals the heart of God. In this sense, his revelation is perfect. That is *not* to say that Jesus exhaustively reveals all there is to know about God, but it *is* to say that, according to Calvinism, Jesus reveals God's love towards humankind in such an exceptional way that there could not be any better way for that love to be revealed. This revelation satisfies everyone who truly comes to know it. The Scottish Calvinist, Thomas Boston, captured something of this sense of satisfaction when he said about the believer's feelings towards Jesus:

> There is nothing in him they would have out of him, and nothing out of him they would have in him.

But here two problems will be obvious to the perceptive reader. One is that the Bible by itself could, it is possible, be as impotent as natural revelation. The second problem was raised earlier: if God is so remarkably different from us, how does the Bible's revelation of God manage to bridge this difference?

To answer the second problem, the Reformed tradition has made considerable use of an ancient idea known as divine accommodation. Divine accommodation refers to God stooping down (so to speak) to communicate with human beings in ways that they can understand, like a mother cooing to her baby. Two thinkers within the Reformed tradition, John Calvin and Klaas Schilder, a Dutch minister and professor at Kampen Seminary who died in 1952, have made extensive use of the notion of divine accommodation in explaining the character of God's revelation—thus, reminding us again of the limited character of 'our theology'.

The Reformed tradition has answered the first problem by proposing a connection between the Word and Spirit of God. For Calvinists, God reveals himself through the Bible in such a way that he ensures this revelation will overcome the impotency that hampered natural revelation. This overcoming is accomplished by God's Spirit causing the message of the scriptures to be truly and really learned by people. The effects of Adam's fall are remedied by this work of the Spirit, and people believe the biblical message.

So, supernatural theology is, it would appear, the property of Christians alone. It is, as John 6:45 states, 'taught by God', which Calvin explains by saying that when God teaches 'through the grace of the Spirit, he so teaches that whatever anyone has learned he not only sees by knowing, but also seeks by willing, and achieves by doing'.

Of course, no Calvinist denies that an atheist can be extremely learned about the contents of the Bible or about the life of Jesus Christ and the history of the church—and most Reformed theologians are willing to call this expertise 'knowledge'. And yet in a more profound sense the Reformed tradition has usually sought to clarify the fact that theological knowledge is of a particular kind; it is what older writers were accustomed to call *effectual* knowledge. It is, we might say, knowledge that belongs to the heart and not merely to the mind. And this kind of knowledge is only possessed by believers to whom God has revealed himself.

But a third problem seems to arise here. Reformed theology says God's revelation is found in the Bible, but we might ask: why should people believe *it* is God's truth? What might someone from a distant un-Christianized land see in the Bible that persuades them that it is revelation from God?

To this question, Calvinists have traditionally argued that the Bible possesses proof of its own divine authorship within itself. Now, this is not what it might seem. The Calvinist's position here might sound like circular reasoning. But Reformed thinkers, such as William Cunningham, who was Professor of Theology at New College, University of Edinburgh, which opened its doors in 1843 (Figure 6) and taught many Reformed theologians, including B. B. Warfield and John Murray, do *not* assert that we know the Bible is God's Word because it says it is and we should believe it when it says this because it is the Word of God. *That* would be circular reasoning. But the Reformed position

6. New College, established in 1843 and now part of Edinburgh University.

is more sophisticated. It says, in its simplest form, that the scriptures contain signs (indications or distinguishing traits) which objectively demonstrate that these writings have God for their author.

The natural question to ask here is, of course, if this is true, then why do only *some* people seem to be able to see these distinguishing marks? Why doesn't everyone see them, if they are objectively present? Here Reformed theologians have answered by reiterating what has been alluded to in the last several paragraphs, namely, that the proofs of the Bible's divine origins are there for all the world to see, but that they cannot be seen because of human blindness, which is caused by Adam's fall—only those whose eyes are opened by the Spirit of God (who are 'taught by God') can see these signs.

Biblical authority

Lingering in the back of our minds may well be a more cynical question. We might be tempted to ask whether Reformed theologians living today believe the Spirit of God somehow makes

Christians trust the Bible and simply overlook the issue of historical accuracy. After all, has it not now been proven that the contents of scripture are historically unreliable?

This is, however, not what the Reformed tradition believes. It believes the Bible *is* historically accurate—an utterly and completely reliable source for knowledge about Jesus, God, the history of the early church, and salvation.

In arguing their position, Calvinists point not so much to the Bible's own claims about itself but rather to archaeological evidence and to the evidence provided by ancient manuscripts. Thousands of manuscripts exist of the Old Testament and, particularly, the New Testament books, which have allowed scholars to put together an extremely reliable copy of the Bible. Thus, the arguments for the reliability and veracity of the Bible made more than a century ago by figures such as B. B. Warfield and A. A. Hodge in answer to the claims of men like F. C. Baur and Julius Wellhausen have continued in the late 20th and into the 21st century to be reworked, refined, and reasserted by Reformed scholars like John Murray, Francis Schaeffer, Carl F. H. Henry, Roger Nicole, R. C. Sproul, Norman Geisler, J. I. Packer, James Montgomery Boice, John Frame, Kevin Vanhoozer, and Richard Bauckham.

These are complex issues and are treated as such by many within the Reformed tradition. Even within the tradition itself there are disagreements on how to interpret the available evidence. Debate exists on various issues, for instance: precisely what it means to say the Bible is accurate or 'inerrant', whether everything in the Bible is stated with scientific precision (the obvious example being the creation account in Genesis 1 and 2), how to understand textual variants found in the biblical books, the identity of the human authors of the Bible, and other issues. But these, most theologians would agree, are matters of interpretation over which disagreements are to be expected.

Chapter 6
Covenant

A covenant is a kind of agreement, treaty, or testament. There are different kinds of covenants that stipulate different obligations, but in the main a covenant is an agreement that binds two parties in a contractual relationship.

The covenant idea is ubiquitous in Reformed thought, so Robert Rollock, a Presbyterian minister and theologian who in 1586 became the first principal of the University of Edinburgh, explained: 'The whole of God's word has to do with some covenant, for God does not communicate to man unless it be through a covenant.' The same point could easily have come from the writings of Ulrich Zwingli, Johannes Cocceius, Hermann Witsius, Patrick Fairbairn, Geerhardus Vos, or a host of modern Reformed authors like Meredith Kline, O. Palmer Robertson, or Michael Horton.

Calvinists speak about God's *one* covenant, but invariably begin identifying a number of interrelated covenants as they explain their thinking further. There are numerous ways the Reformed tradition speaks about these covenants, which we will explore by making use of the helpful breakdown found in the writings of Donald MacLeod.

The covenant of redemption

Covenant theologians speak about a covenant which they believe was entered into before God created anything. It is a covenant between the members of the Trinity: the Father, the Son, and the Holy Spirit. They refer to it as an eternal covenant. In it, God the Father and God the Son covenanted with one another, such that the Son agreed to become a man, obey, suffer, and die in the place of his (as yet uncreated) people, the elect. The Father, in return, promised the Son salvation, which the Son would then give to the elect.

Reformed thinking that supports the idea of this covenant rests on biblical passages (Psalm 2:7–9, for example) but equally on theological considerations. As Donald MacLeod explains: 'Scripture constantly relates Christ's mission to the will of God the Father. He was sent from God, received his rules of engagement from God and received certain promises from God. Such language', MacLeod observes, 'clearly indicates that he did not come on his own initiative alone, but on terms agreed with the Father.' A covenant agreement was also necessary for the union between Christ and his people. The Father could not simply have decreed that Christ be united with his people, as that could well mean that Christ's obedience on their behalf would have been involuntary. Thus, this union between them must have been decided by, and based on, the covenant of redemption.

The idea of a covenant of redemption is not an idea with which all the Reformed agree. It is thought by some that the thinking contained within it could have been included in the next two covenants.

The covenant of works

This covenant (sometimes called the covenant of life or covenant of nature) was made between God and Adam. In it God imposed conditions on Adam, which he was required to obey and would receive a reward for doing so.

Although this covenant was between God and Adam, Adam was not regarded as a private individual. Rather, he represented all humankind. Thus, were he to render perfect obedience to this covenant's stipulations, which focused on *not* eating the fruit of the tree of the knowledge of good and evil (Genesis 2:16–17) found in the Garden of Eden, he would be rewarded with eternal life for both himself and his posterity. Likewise, disobedience would bring death to all.

This covenant is not explicitly mentioned in Genesis, the biblical book that records the story of the fall of Adam and Eve, though Calvinists believe it is implied there. But they contend that its theological details are explained in the Apostle Paul's letters in the New Testament, specifically, Romans 5. There Paul speaks of death reigning 'even over those who did not sin by breaking a command, as did Adam'. Paul also speaks of Adam as 'a type' of the one to come—meaning, Jesus Christ.

The probationary aspect of this covenant is no longer applicable to people today. Adam stood, as already mentioned, in the place of all humankind and broke the terms of this contract for all. Yet, this covenant is still in force in one sense. The Bible declares, 'Do this and live!' (Galatians 3:12) meaning that if someone were to obey God perfectly, she could merit salvation. The problem is that human sinfulness makes such perfect obedience impossible.

The covenant of grace

While non-Christians live under the death sentence merited by Adam under the covenant of work, Christians live under the covenant of grace, in which Adam's role as head has been taken over by Jesus Christ. Here 1 Corinthians 15:45 leads the way: 'The first man Adam became a living soul. The last Adam became a life-giving spirit.' The clarity of this biblical passage helps provide a sense of the relationship between the two covenants, and underscores the notion that Jesus came to win back for the elect what was lost in Adam; to do for them what they could not do for themselves.

Despite its clarity, it has been difficult for covenant theologians neatly and unambiguously to identify details related to this covenant or, even, precisely who the parties making the covenant are. In fact, if one is not careful in his thinking, he finds that he has effectively erased any difference between the covenant of grace and the covenant of redemption. In clarifying Reformed thinking on this impasse, MacLeod's observation is, again, helpful:

> What is needed here is a firm commitment to seeing the covenant of grace in terms of the Abrahamic covenant (recorded in Genesis 17). Abraham was not Christ (or even a type of Christ). Nor was the covenant made with him as elect. Nor, again, was it made with him before time began. It was made with him, in history, as a believer; and this warrants the conclusion that the parties in the covenant of grace are God on the one hand and the believer on the other.

This would also appear to be the view taken by someone like Caspar Olevianus, the German Reformer, and also the two Scottish theologians, David Dickson and Samuel Rutherford. Dickson's *The Sum of Saving Knowledge* and *Therapeutica Sacra* are both worthy of acknowledgement here.

The covenant of grace is understood by Reformed theology as promising eternal life. It is ordinarily held that faith is the condition that needs to be met to receive eternal life, but precisely how that is understood can vary considerably. On the one hand, the gospel has to be understood as free. God's love and grace are not merited by someone fulfilling the stipulations of the covenant.

But on the other hand, human beings are required to respond to God's gospel call. This response is utterly real and meaningful. Thus, faith is a requirement but not a condition.

Lest someone think that the covenant of grace applies only for those living after Jesus's death and resurrection, Reformed theologians have made it extremely clear that this covenant applies to every believer, both in the Old Testament and the New Testament eras. Calvinists teach that men and women like Adam, Abraham, Sarah, Ruth, Deborah, David, Elijah, and Jeremiah were believers in fundamentally the same way as New Testament Christians.

Accordingly, Calvinists talk about the one covenant of grace as having two 'administrations'—it has an administration during the period of history prior to the coming of Jesus Christ and a new administration that was introduced with Christ's resurrection and the giving of the Spirit on the day of Pentecost. But both are manifestations of the covenant of grace through which God saves his elect people.

These two administrations differ in ways which are reflective of the spiritual maturity of the two covenant communities. So, Calvinists argue that those living before Christ were spiritually immature compared with their New Testament counterparts. The relevant biblical text here is Galatians 4:1–3, which depicts the covenant community during the Old Testament era as adolescents (as opposed to being adults). Now, both communities have a sign that is applied to those under the covenant. During the Old Testament period, that sign was circumcision. With the New Testament era, the sign changed to baptism. But the reality pointed to by these signs is the same.

More recently, some Reformed theologians have criticized traditional thought on the covenants. For example, the graciousness of God's approach is believed, by some, to have been lost through thinking about the conditions of the covenant, which is interpreted as introducing 'legalism' into God's dealings with his people. John Murray, who taught at Westminster Theological Seminary, expressed his dislike for the idea of the covenant of works, which, he complained, obscures the graciousness of God's covenant with Adam. Some, such as G. C. Berkouwer of the Free University of Amsterdam and also J. B. Torrance, the long-time Professor of Dogmatics at the University of Aberdeen, wrote with disdain about the whole idea of 'federal' theology—covenant theology is sometimes called federal theology or federalism, after the Latin word, *foedus*, which means covenant. Torrance found it to be legalistic and a departure from the true theology of John Calvin.

A kind of revival of covenant theology has recently appeared through the rise of the Federal Vision, also known as Auburn Avenue theology, though not without controversy. Doug Wilson and Steve Wilkins, leaders within this movement, teach that God's covenant (referring effectively to God's covenant of grace) is objective. They join together divine election, covenant membership, and baptism and argue that 'we are to view election through the lens of the covenant'. In simple terms, that means that if someone is a covenant member then the blessings of the covenant belong to them. The covenant becomes a lens through which the Christian life is to be considered. Personal assurance of salvation, for instance, is to be considered through baptism (i.e. through the act that places a person into the covenant) and *not* through the kinds of self-examination we discussed in Chapter 2. Federal Vision adherents insist that they fall comfortably within the range of different takes on covenant theology that have been developed over the centuries, but others such as Guy Waters, R. Scott Clark, John Fesko, and David VanDrunen disagree. Though an American debate, the issues it addresses are universally important.

God predestines (and reprobates)

Basic to Calvinist conceptions of knowing God, and central to
the idea of the covenant of grace, is God's work of predestination.
This doctrine is infamously associated with Calvinism, but in
actual fact the views of Calvin, Theodore Beza, Jerome Zanchi,
and a myriad of other Reformed theologians were taught, in the
main, by Augustine 1,000 years earlier. Thus, the doctrine of
predestination is not a Calvinist creation. Some have argued that
Augustine did not teach the related doctrine of reprobation (which
many Calvinists teach), though a strong argument can be made
that he did.

But what do these ideas mean and how do Calvinists understand
them? Let me begin with a brief word on divine providence.
Divine providence relates to God's governing of all things; that is,
his deciding, or willing, or (the theological term usually used)
decreeing of all things. God decrees all things to happen, that is,
quite literally every single thing that ever happens. This includes
all sins and disasters too: an earthquake in Turkey as well as the
murder of an elderly woman beloved by her entire village. Most
significantly, this includes the murder of Jesus Christ, God's Son.

There is an obvious moral question associated with God decreeing
something like murder, which is a sin. The earliest Reformed
thinkers had few, if any, qualms about this. Emphasizing divine
power, they declared that God willed all things, evil included, yet
in such a manner that God's holiness was not tarnished in any
way. They used biblical passages like Job 1:21, 'the Lord gives and
the Lord takes away', to defend their position. A nice example of
this teaching is found in Jerome Zanchi's *Absolute Predestination*.
Later Reformed theologians exhibit more caution. They feel
happier speaking about God's decree when it is safeguarded by a
distinction, which treats decrees of evil differently from other
decrees. Louis Berkhof, for example, who taught on the faculty of

Calvin Theological Seminary for nearly forty years, declared: 'It is customary to speak of the decree of God respecting moral evil as *permissive*.'

A pastoral concern motivates theologians like Berkhof here. The idea of a permissive decree seeks to clarify God's hatred of all moral evil. Some of the New Calvinists (or Neo-Puritans), such as John Piper, however, have returned to the attitudes of early thinkers, emphasizing God's utter sovereignty. Irrespective of the approach taken to this specific issue, Calvinists insist that God controls all things meticulously and that God's people derive unspeakable comfort from the fact that even the worst things in the world are under God's control and are, therefore, incapable of ultimately harming them. 'If God is for us,' the Calvinist says, reciting the words of Romans 8:31, 'who can be against us?'

There is also a question that arises over the compatibility between God's decrees and human freedom. Concerning it, Calvinists have consistently asserted that God's decreeing of all things does not conflict with human free will. Some have preferred simply to contend that both are taught in scripture and therefore ought to be believed for that reason. Others, however, have mounted philosophically oriented defences.

The position most Calvinists defend is known as compatibilism. Defence of compatibilism usually entails restricting what is meant by human *freedom*. So, for example, the compatibilist will argue that people have freedom to act according to their motivations, but they cannot be said to be free in some kind of unrestricted, absolute sense which would allow them to do whatsoever they like, as if they did not have a nature.

Opposing this is a view of human freedom known as libertarianism. It asserts that when a person acts, she can choose from a range of possibilities without the constraints of her nature imposing themselves. Free means uncaused; that is, no event or efficient cause makes her do this thing or that. While the majority of Calvinists adhere to some form of compatibilism, it is not impossible to conceive of a libertarian Calvinist, as Oliver Crisp of Fuller Theological Seminary has recently argued.

A French Jesuit theologian named Luis de Molina, who lived at roughly the same time as Zwingli, Bullinger, and Calvin, proposed a new understanding of the problem of human freedom and divine sovereignty. His understanding has influenced some Calvinist theologians up to the present day. Molina examined the character of God's will, rather than focusing on the question of human freedom. Molinism proposes that God has something called 'middle knowledge', which constitutes God's knowledge of what free human beings *would* do under any set of circumstances. According to Molina, God is able to decree everything that comes to pass without hindering human freedom in any way, because God is able to bring about his will perfectly by knowing what each person would do in a given set of circumstances and using that knowledge to effect his own will.

Turning to the topic of predestination, it should now be clear that it relates intimately to divine providence. Predestination is understood by Reformed theologians as: the eternal decree of God by which all human beings are appointed either to eternal life or to eternal damnation. This is further divided into a decree of election and a decree of reprobation according to which the elect go to heaven and the reprobate to hell. God is utterly free to decree whatever he wishes without any encumbrance or external influence. According to Reformed theology, God does not decree based on foreknowing (i.e. looking into the future in order to discover) that you or I will, or will not, become Christians and *then* decreeing accordingly. Rather, God has determined, for reasons known only to himself, whatever he wishes regarding every man and woman.

The decree of reprobation is understood differently by different Calvinists. In order to examine this difference, we need to consider two theological positions: infralapsarianism and supralapsarianism. These two terms relate to a topic which some might find bizarre, namely, the question of how God ordered (not in temporal order like the steps I might take to bake a cake, but rather logical ordering) his decrees in his mind. Depending on the order of these decrees, we arrive, it is argued by a number of Calvinists, at rather different conceptions of God's character.

In the infralapsarian model, the decrees are ordered logically as: (1) create the human race; (2) authorize the fall of Adam; (3) elect some from the fallen race (from the 'corrupt mass') to salvation and pass over the rest; (4) provide for the salvation of the elect through Jesus Christ. Under this arrangement, God predestines people from *sinful* humanity, *after* the fall has been decreed. There is, then, not a specific decree of reprobation, since it is not needed; God's authorizing of the fall set the necessary circumstances in place. Accordingly, some refer to this as single predestination.

In the supralapsarian model, the decrees are ordered logically as: (1) elect some and reprobate others from as-yet-uncreated humanity, all for the revealing of God's glory; (2) create the human race; (3) authorize the fall of Adam; (4) provide for salvation of the elect through Jesus Christ. Under this arrangement, God is understood to elect and to reprobate; hence, double predestination. These decrees *precede* the fall. Therefore, rather than merely passing over those in the corrupt mass whom he does not choose to elect to salvation, God deliberately reprobates some to damnation. So, God decides to save and damn and then determines the means by which these aims will be accomplished.

One can espouse double predestination without speculating on the ordering of the decrees in God's mind. Calvin might possibly be pointed to as someone who did this. However, he makes occasional speculative comments in his writings which could be interpreted as linking him to either of these two models, but he never speaks to the question explicitly. Indeed, it had not yet become a question. It became a question and, in fact, a heated topic of debate not long after his death.

Well-known supralapsarians include Calvin's successor in Geneva, Theodore Beza, the 17th-century Scottish minister Samuel Rutherford, and the 20th-century Dutch theologian Herman Hoeksema. Well-known infralapsarians include the English Puritan John Owen, Charles Hodge, the Princeton Seminary professor, and the 20th-century theologian and founder of Ligonier ministries, R. C. Sproul. Some, like Herman Bavinck and Robert Lewis Dabney, believed that the question of the ordering of decrees in God's mind should never have been asked, as it is far too speculative.

Jesus atones for sins

Both the infralapsarian and supralapsarian positions include a decree (specifically, the fourth) to provide salvation for the elect through Jesus Christ; specifically through his coming to die to atone for human sins. Here, Jesus takes on the role of priest. Just as he has been identified as King and Prophet in Chapters 4 and 5, respectively, so Jesus also performs the office of priest, which he executes 'in his once offering up of himself a sacrifice to satisfy divine justice, and reconcile us to God, and in making continual intercession for us', as the *Westminster Shorter Catechism* states.

There are many issues that arise in discussions of the atonement, a complex topic, but one of the more important is the question of who Jesus died for. Who is the 'us' mentioned by the *Shorter Catechism*? This question may seem puzzling. Since the Bible says, 'God so loved that world that he gave his only begotten son', in John 3:16, doesn't that indicate that Jesus died for everyone?

According to most Reformed theologians, the answer is 'no'. Jesus suffered a penal, substitutionary death on behalf of all the elect alone and not for every single human being.

This understanding has been referred to as 'particular redemption' or 'limited atonement'. These names were devised in the 17th century during a meeting of church leaders which aimed to settle a controversy known as the Quinquarticular Controversy (quinquarticular means having to do with five points), which was between Calvinists and a group called Arminians. The controversy was addressed at the Synod of Dordt, in the Netherlands, during the years 1618–19, to which representatives from Reformed churches throughout Europe were invited. These five points raised by those who followed Jacob Arminius (hence the name, Arminians) were called the five 'articles of Remonstrance'. They ended up being rejected by the Reformed churches at the synod.

The *Canons of Dordt*, published after the synod, contain the Five Points of Calvinism, which have been viewed by many as a brilliant summary of what Calvinism teaches about Christian salvation. These points are often referred to by the acronym TULIP, where the T stands for Total Depravity, U for Unconditional Election, L for Limited Atonement, I for Irresistible Grace, and P for Perseverance of the Saints.

Biblical support for limited atonement is found, Calvinists claim, in passages like John 6:37–40 and 1 Corinthians 1:30, both of which seem to speak about Christ's ministry and death as actually *achieving* salvation for a specific group. In John 17, another such passage, Jesus prays to his Father, 'I am not praying for the world but for those whom you have given me, for they are yours', referring (Calvinists say) to the elect. The Reformed also point to texts like Matthew 1:21, which declares that Jesus will 'save *his people* from their sins'. Likewise, in John 10:14–15 Jesus says, 'I lay down my life for *my sheep*'. He then tells a group of people later

(John 10:26), 'you are *not* my sheep'. So Jesus himself, Calvinists insist, plainly asserts the distinction articulated in the doctrine of particular redemption.

When the objection is raised that Jesus died for the 'world' (1 John 2:2) and 'gave his life a ransom for all' (1 Timothy 2:6), Calvinists, such as Christopher Ness, who wrote the brilliantly titled *An Antidote to Arminianism*, explain that scripture often uses words like 'world' and 'all' in limited senses. They point to texts like Luke 2:1, which states that Caesar Augustus decreed 'that all the world should be registered', and explain that 'all' and 'world' here cannot mean every individual human being.

Another objection levelled against limited atonement complains that if Christ's death paid for the sins of the elect, then this seems to make the atonement into a kind of commercial transaction. The debt is pecuniary and payment frees the debtor *ipso facto*. To be sure, there are Calvinists and (actually) Arminians who hold this position, but it is not commonly taught by Calvinists. Most Calvinists distinguish between penal and moral satisfaction, on the one hand, and pecuniary payment, on the other. Christ's atonement represents the former. The benefits of Christ's atoning death are applied to the elect 'only at God's discretion and according to God's purposes', as Oliver Crisp recently clarified in his *Deviant Calvinism*. God has purposed that it will be applied to believers through his Spirit working in the hearts of the elect to draw them to Jesus. Thus, the atonement is not commercial.

Reformed views on the penal nature of Christ's atonement have been criticized for making God appear vengeful. Calvinists dispute this charge, contending that retribution is not the same as vengeance. God's fundamental judgement, as Robert Lewis Dabney and countless others have said, is 'that sin is to be punished *because it deserves to be*'. Impartial justice requires due penalty and demands reward for virtue.

There are some theologians who agree with the other four points of Calvinism, but do not accept particular redemption. Many of them embrace a position called Amyraldianism, named after Moïse Amyraut. Amyraldianism teaches a form of hypothetical universalism. This means that it teaches the universal death of Christ for all human beings, which is then applied particularly to the elect. It is applied particularly by God because he foresees that there will be some who reject Christ's death.

This position operates on a view of the atonement articulated during the Middle Ages and reiterated by various Protestant reformers, including Bullinger and Calvin. The view is expressed in the slogan: 'Jesus died sufficiently for all men and efficiently only for the elect.' It highlights the fact—which no one questions—that the virtue of the death of Jesus Christ must surely be infinite and easily sufficient for each and every person.

Hypothetical universalism has at least two benefits, its proponents claim. First, it places greater emphasis on God's mercy and lovingkindness by depicting the death of Jesus as universal in scope. It is ordinarily interpreted as laying greater weight, as regards the cause of someone ending up in hell, upon those who reject that death. Second, it enables one to read passages like John 3:16 in what is argued by some to be a more natural way. Hypothetical universalism was held by important Calvinists like Richard Baxter and J. C. Ryle. What John Calvin himself taught on the atonement has been disputed for years. The classic statement on particular redemption is John Owen's *The Death of Death in the Death of Christ*, which runs to an intimidating 283 pages (of tiny print). Few subjects have been debated more vigorously.

Lurking behind all that we have covered in this chapter is the topic of love. The Reformed understanding of the covenants, divine predestination, and the atoning work of Christ plainly sets out a particular interpretation of God's love. 'God is love' as we read in 1 John 4:8. For Calvinism, God is free to do as he pleases, and has freely chosen to love and commit himself to his elect with whom he covenants. But this interpretation leaves open some tantalizing questions, to which we will return in Chapter 8.

Chapter 7
Humanity and new humanity

Just after 4.10 p.m. on 14 August 2003, New York City was plunged into darkness due to a power outage. The widespread looting and mayhem that commenced continued for hours, until the electricity was restored.

Why is a blackout the occasion for such behaviour? The answer is surely complex. Yet events such as this one serve, Calvinists suggest, to illustrate the deep disorder and corruption of the human heart. Calvinism teaches that human beings possess within themselves evil desires that are suppressed through domesticating influences such as laws and social norms, and unleashed when these influences are removed. In this way, Calvinism bears a fascinating resemblance to Freudianism. Both teach that aggressive and sexual forces are hidden deep inside the minds of all human beings and that if these are not controlled they would lead individuals and societies to chaos and destruction. Thus, when the blackout occurred, the hidden drives present deep within were unleashed.

This is a dour, depressing view of humanity, to be sure. But Calvinism argues it is an accurate one. It gets a lot of bad press for doing so, but with humankind's seemingly endless capacity to shock, we cannot really laugh too loudly at Calvinists if their view of humankind seeks to reflect that reality.

Original sin

Very few ideas have impacted the Reformed tradition as deeply as the idea of original sin, which resulted from the fall of Adam and Eve. The fall of Adam and Eve is believed to have occurred in the Garden of Eden. The story is recorded in Genesis 3, the most tragic portion of which reads:

> When the woman saw that the fruit of the tree was good for food and pleasing to the eye, and also desirable for gaining wisdom, she took some and ate it. She also gave some to her husband, who was with her, and he ate it. Then the eyes of both of them were opened, and they realized they were naked.

Despite exhibiting considerable variety of opinion on a host of questions related to the age of the earth and other scientifically oriented matters, most Calvinists believe that Adam and Eve were historical persons and that the fall really occurred, though it is not inconceivable that some might choose to recast the event in terms of an original hominid community.

According to Reformed teachings, Adam and Eve had been created in God's image. A complex topic, this image is generally understood by Calvinists to relate to spiritual qualities like righteousness and justice. Thus, the Reformed believe that Adam and Eve had been granted innumerable blessings (including original righteousness), the greatest being friendship with God, and they lost them.

Calvinism teaches that as a result of the fall, Adam and Eve lost original righteousness both for themselves and for their posterity. Thus, because of the fall, three things are true of every baby brought into the world. They are guilty before God. They have an inborn propensity to sin. And, they still possess something of the image of God, though that image is seriously tarnished.

Reformed beliefs on the fall and its effects derive primarily from two sources. First, the Bible—not only the passage already cited from Genesis, but also the writings of the Apostle Paul, especially his letter to the Romans. In chapter 5 of that letter, he writes: 'through one man sin entered into the world, and death through sin, and so death spread to all men, because all sinned' (Romans 5:12; this 'one man' is, the chapter makes clear, Adam). And the second source for these Reformed beliefs is the theology of Augustine. His theology had an enormous impact on Reformed thought, and nowhere is this more apparent than in thinking on human sinfulness.

Although Calvinists agree that Adam's sin affected all his descendants, they explain the transmission of his sin in different ways. One common way Calvinists explain how Adam's sin was passed down to humankind involves the idea of representation. Just as elected officials represent their constituents and the actions of these officials can influence the constituents whom they represent, so it was with Adam. Adam was believed by these theologians to be the covenant or federal (from the Latin, *foedus*, which means covenant) head of the human race, and therefore his conduct had an impact on all humanity.

A common complaint about this idea of representation is that humankind did not have the opportunity to choose their own representative. Perhaps they would have chosen a better one? After all, who chose Adam? There was no vote, and yet humanity is saddled with problems arising directly from him. The answer usually given to this complaint by Calvinists is that *God* made the choice and that, because it is what he willed, it must be regarded as best. A second complaint could be made, which focuses on precisely how corruption could be imputed to those whom Adam represented. The corrupting of a person's nature through the means of representation seems, to some, extremely hard to explain and to justify.

There are, however, other ways that Reformed theologians have explained the transmission of Adam's sin to his posterity. One of these other explanations is found in the theology of Ulrich Zwingli. Precisely what Zwingli believed on this subject is disputed, but it would appear that he denied that Adam's *guilt* is passed down to his descendants. Adam's *corruption* is still transmitted to them, but people are not *guilty* before God until they themselves actually sin. Part of Zwingli's reasoning here, it would appear, was to keep someone from objecting that it was irrevocably fated that he or she would go to hell, since they were already guilty before they performed even a single act of their own. Zwingli's solution has the merit of making a person's guilt be based on their own conduct, rather than on the conduct of a representative.

One of the more fascinating alternatives to the federal representation scheme is the position held by the American Calvinist theologian and philosopher, Jonathan Edwards. Edwards based his understanding on two theological beliefs. First, he held to a doctrine of continuous creation. This means that the existence of all things at all times is the immediate effect of God's power. Though this may seem a slightly odd belief for a theologian to have, Edwards developed it with particular concerns in mind that were part of his contemporary situation. The idea that God was continually creating everything that we see around us offered him a way of affirming God's active presence in the universe over against the rising belief in the 18th century of Deism, which contended that God created the universe and set universal laws in place, but subsequently allowed it to continue on its own without interference—like a watchmaker, who makes a watch and then allows it to run on its own.

Second, Edwards held that our own personal identity must be understood in light of the doctrine of continuous creation. He used these two beliefs to interpret the doctrine of original sin, and particularly the notion that Adam's sin could justly be transferred to his posterity. This Edwards did so as to refute an objection that it was simply unjust for God to apply Adam's sin to anyone else. Adam and his posterity, the objector explains, are plainly not the same person and therefore it is immoral to associate the sins of this one man with those who came after him. But Edwards argued that in a real sense Adam and his posterity were not wholly distinct and unrelated; they were in a sense one man. The sin of Adam is, Edwards contended, truly ascribed to Adam's descendants because, by a divinely constituted identity, Adam and all his posterity *are* one moral person. Thus, Edwards wanted to argue, *we all* sinned with Adam.

Despite the existence of various explanations, by the 19th century two main Reformed positions had emerged: federalism, which relies, as we have seen, on representation, and realism, which depends on the unity that exists between Adam and his posterity, such that they are viewed as present in Adam when he sinned (and therefore his sin is imputed to them). Both bring us to the notion that people are born slaves to sin.

Slaves to sin

'He is most perfect who condemns himself the most.' John Calvin spoke these cheery words to his congregation at St Pierre Cathedral in Geneva in the summer of 1555. His assertion, which comes from a sermon he preached on Deuteronomy 7:11–15, brilliantly conveys the seriousness ascribed by the Reformed to the fall and its ramifications, according to which humankind are factories spewing out corruption.

But the infection passed down through the imputing of Adam's sin does not only mean human beings are bad in some general sense. It means they are born enslaved to sin. This teaching of Calvinism is represented by the T in the acronym associated with Dutch Calvinism, TULIP. The T of course stands for Total Depravity.

In this day and age, the word 'slavery' carries with it profoundly disturbing connotations, which underscore the seriousness of this plight. Calvinism really does regard the state of humankind as dire. It, therefore, comes as no surprise to the Calvinist when Jeremiah 17:9 declares, 'the heart is more deceitful than all else, and is desperately sick; who can understand it?'

Calvinism teaches that this is a willing enslavement. In other words, it is not as if people are held captive to sin *against* their wills. Rather, the enslavement is precisely an enslavement of a person's will. People love sin. They *want* to sin. No one forces them to sin; it is what they desire.

But here a common objection is raised. In addition to simply seeming unfair, people object that this teaching is contradicted by experience. After all, we see people do good things every day.

The Reformed tradition responds by acknowledging that people are able to perform acts that are apparently virtuous, they know right from wrong, and so forth. Yet while acknowledging this, the Reformed tradition sticks to its guns, insisting that moral corruption stains every part of human nature so deeply that everyone is potentially Pol Pot, Myra Hindley, or Joseph Stalin, and that what we see when we see people doing good is, in fact, a deception. It suggests people are good, when they actually are not.

People know, the Reformed tradition insists, that there is a God; they cannot escape this knowledge, which is innate and extremely powerful. People also feel the kinds of pressures associated with civil law and social norms and expectations that we briefly mentioned when discussing the New York City blackout. And, feeling these pressures, they subconsciously alter their behaviour, masking their sinful desires under a veneer of civility.

The rejoinder of some is to say that while there are *some* bad people, there are also many who are good; Calvinism's tarring of everyone with the same brush is wrong. But the Reformed insist that there are depths of evil in even the most ordinary individuals. This is brilliantly illustrated in Daniel Goldhagen's 1996 study, *Hitler's Willing Executioners*. Goldhagen demonstrates how ordinary Germans rose up to serve within the Nazi programme, acting in ways they would have thought unimaginable before Hitler came to power. Goldhagen's book is, the Calvinist contends, not an indictment of Germans but of every human being. It is an indictment of the human heart.

Now, both the restraining of sin and the escape from enslavement to sin are things Calvinists explain by pointing to the idea of grace. The subject is often divided in two, with common grace referring to God's restraining work and special grace his work of freeing someone from enslavement to sin. We have already discussed common grace in Chapter 3, but will return to it briefly here.

Grace

Grace is, as Louis Berkhof asserts, 'that perfection of God in virtue of which he shows unmerited and even forfeited favour to man'. *Common* grace involves God showing kindness to people; kindness that does *not* result in people being converted but that does still have a profound effect. It functions to bless people in various ways and especially to restrain human sinfulness.

The idea of common grace was devised by Calvinists to account for why people who are slaves to sin still do good; why sinful people still have remarkable abilities, such as the ability to compose beautiful music or to be a brilliant scientist; why a society full of horribly sinful people functions properly.

Reformed theology teaches that common grace is shown by God to everyone, the elect and the non-elect (Matthew 5:45, 'God causes his rain to fall on the righteous and the sinful'). It is categorized by a theologian like Berkhof under three heads:

(1) Universal Common Grace: a grace that extends to all creatures; (2) General Common Grace: a grace which applies to humankind in general and to every member of the human race; (3) Covenant Common Grace: a grace that is common to all those who live in the sphere of the covenant (i.e. within the church), whether they belong to the elect or not.

The idea of common grace seems to have first been explicitly discussed by John Calvin in his *Institutes of the Christian Religion*. It was developed further by Abraham Kuyper, the Dutch theologian, politician, newspaper editor, and minister, who spoke about it in various publications such as his *Common Grace* and also *Lectures on Calvinism*, which he delivered at Princeton Theological Seminary in 1898.

Common grace has, however, garnered criticism from some within the Reformed community, probably most vociferously from Herman Hoeksema, a Dutch theologian who pastored a church in Grand Rapids, Michigan for many years. Others who questioned it, to various degrees, or constructed novel understandings of it include Klaas Schilder, David Engelsma (a student of Hoeksema), S. G. De Graaf, Cornelius Van Til, William Masselink, and James Daane.

This criticism often focuses on what the objector believes is an inappropriate use of the word, 'grace'. Common grace, Hoeksema complains, suggests that God is actually favourable towards the unbelieving world, when in fact God expresses intense anger towards unbelievers (Psalm 7:10–12; 11:4–6; 145:20). The Bible, he and others insist, reserves the word 'grace' for communications of God's love and mercy as expressed in his gospel and is ultimately reserved for God's elect alone. Thus, to use the word to discuss God's kindness to unbelievers is wrong.

God's *special* grace, by contrast, is reserved for his elect. If God has elected a person to salvation, he will at some point favour them with his special grace which will bring about their conversion. It is this, Calvinists believe, the Bible is referring to in, for instance, Ephesians 2:8: 'For it is by grace you have been saved.' This teaching of Calvinism is represented by the I in the TULIP acronym, Irresistible Grace.

The basic sense of what happens when God visits someone with special grace is that he breaks the resistance that person had been showing God up to that point. She who was a slave to her sin is now overcome by God's love. Her heart is changed, and she begins to love God. So Acts 16:14 declares of Lydia, a seller of purple fabric who was listening to the Apostle Paul preach, that 'the Lord opened her heart to respond to Paul's message'. And Romans 8:30 explains that those whom God predestined, he also 'called'. This call is, Calvinists believe, effectual; it achieves its aim. It is irresistible.

The instrumental means through which this change is facilitated is ordinarily the preaching of the gospel, as was the case with Lydia. Although many people will hear this preaching and go away unchanged, a different result awaits God's elect, who will hear the message of the gospel and believe it.

This work is accomplished by the Spirit of God. It is a real change in the person. It is not a bodily change. It causes no physiological or neurological changes to take place. It is also not something that changes the person so radically that she is now completely rid of all sin. The reign of sin in her life has been broken, but during her time on this earth from her conversion until the day she dies, she will always, according to Calvinism, struggle with sin. Only in heaven will all sinful desires be removed from her heart.

This is a sovereign work of God and does not involve cooperation by the individual. Just to be precise, let us say the person herself does act; that is, she *believes*. She believes in the gospel. She uses her intellect to understand what she hears in the preaching of the gospel. She uses her will in choosing to believe the message she hears. So she is active. But all her activity (all her believing) is the result *entirely* of God's free and sovereign work. God initiates and at the time he does this, the recipient of his grace is not cooperating with God but is, in fact, wholly opposed to God, as all people are prior to conversion.

Once someone is converted through God's special grace, God makes them his child. Calvinism teaches she has been adopted (Romans 8:14–15), justified before God (Romans 3–5; i.e. she is not guilty before God any more, but is regarded as innocent), and will be glorified (Romans 8:30).

But how can God's gracious work be irresistible? Plainly many people resist God's message. Yet Calvinists teach that when God works through his Spirit in the heart of one of his elect, he produces a change akin to correcting someone's vision. Now that they can see God for who he really is, they cannot help but love him. The perfect beauty of God is such that if anyone is released from their enslavement to sin (which blinds them from seeing God's beauty), they will be unable to resist that beauty.

New life

Having become a Christian, the convert lives a new life in covenant relationship with God. To describe the Reformed approach to life, we might start off on a sanguine note. When life is peaceful and devoid of problems, Calvinism teaches the cultivation of thankfulness. This is a major theme of Puritan manuals of piety like Henry Scudder's *The Christian's Daily Walk*, Robert Bolton's *General Directions for a Comfortable Walking with God*, and Lewis Bayly's *The Practice of Piety*.

When facing difficulty, suffering, and discouragement, Calvinism teaches the Christian to understand that God brings this as well. So, the 17th-century Anglican, John Preston, encourages his congregation 'to think the Lord hath put me into this condition; he might have given me strength to goe abroad as others doe, but hee hath laid sickness upon me'. Facing such troubles, the Christian does not curse God, nor does she say 'this is *not* the work of God; God would never do such a thing, etc.' Rather she understands: 'when times are good, be happy; but when times are bad, consider: God has made the one as well as the other' (Ecclesiastes 7:14).

This belief that God brings troubles has led to Calvinism being harshly criticized for depicting God as a monster. But Calvinists don't see it that way. For the Calvinist, God *because he is God* must be in charge of all things. Calvinism insists that the greatest possible comfort is found in understanding that all things are governed by the God who has chosen the Christian before she was born and will ensure that nothing can take her out of God's hand. He will make sure she makes it through the trials of this life and will comfort her through all of them. So, when facing difficulties, the Calvinist declares with Job: 'though God slay me, yet will I trust in him' (Job 13:15).

Essential to this new life is prayer, which Calvinists speak of with utter assurance precisely *because* their God controls all things. No one speaks more confidently about prayer than John Calvin, who refers regularly in his sermons to the utter certainty Christians ought to have that God will answer their prayers. Ministers like Calvin, John Bunyan, and Charles Spurgeon describe prayer as the truest expression of the Christian religion.

In good times and bad, Calvinists strive to remain faithful to God. To do this, they have adopted a distinction found in the theology of Augustine, who distinguishes between 'use' (the Latin Augustine uses is *uti*) and 'enjoyment' (*frui*). Enjoyment, as the term is used here, means to love something for its own sake or (as they say) as an end in itself. Use, by contrast, means to love something for the sake of some other thing or as a means to a higher end. The distinction might seem slightly odd, but Calvinists have found it very useful. It provides guidance as to how to live in this world.

Reformed theology says that God alone deserves to be enjoyed (*frui*). He is the only thing who is properly regarded as an ultimate end. Thus, the Christian should find in God her delight and ultimate meaning. With respect to everything else, Calvinism teaches that it should be appreciated, but in a different way. It should be used (*uti*) as a means to the higher purpose of loving God. Thus, everything—from your job to a nice glass of wine to your husband and your favourite hobby—is to be loved for God's sake and not as an end in itself. They are all gifts from God. They reflect God's love and generosity and beauty. But they should not be regarded as ends. Rather, the Christian should love them for the sake of God.

This may seem extraordinarily restrictive, but it is actually believed by Calvinists to be liberating. What it indicates is that everything in this world can be used as a means to know God better. A person doesn't have to sit in church to learn to love God more deeply. She can do that anywhere with anything. This point is made by the English Puritan, Richard Baxter, who (famously) said that through a skilful use of the things of this world, 'we might have a fuller taste of Christ and heaven, in every bit of bread that we eat, and in every draught of beer that we drink, than most men have in the use of the sacrament'. Whether the Calvinist is cleaning her office or fishing, she is able to benefit spiritually from the experience. The kind of meditations found in John Flavel's *The Mystery of Providence* bring this out brilliantly.

Now, Calvinism does *not* suggest here a simplistic understanding according to which the Christian never has her mind on the task at hand but rather must somehow attempt to extricate herself from that task and meditate on God instead. Calvinism does not teach or imply that every task or every thing is evil or empty or a waste of time. On the contrary, it teaches that the activities that fill human life ought to be thoroughly enjoyed, being understood as gifts from a loving Father who wants his people to learn about him through those gifts. So, a child will find even more delight in a new toy *because* it is a gift to her from her father, whom she loves even more intensely because of his gift.

Equally liberating, within this *uti–frui* distinction, is the Reformed understanding of work. During the Protestant Reformation, Lutherans and Calvinists engaged in a momentous re-evaluation of the meaning of human labour. They argued that people can serve God through work of many different kinds, and not just, as had previously been argued by Roman Catholicism, through serving God as a priest or a nun. People, these Protestants contended, have God-given talents that should be used in the service of God and neighbour. All of life, they argued, is a series of callings dictated by the circumstances in which God places the individual Christian.

Human circumstances are not accidents but are preordained by God and to be understood as the arenas within which the Christian serves God. This ought, it is said, to liberate the Christian, allowing her to pour her energies and talents into whatever she does knowing that God will receive her work as good service done for his glory and the good of God's kingdom.

In lifestyle, Calvinists have a reputation for being prudish and repressive, but the reality is different. They aim to be circumspect and godly, but precisely what this looks like varies according to time, geography, and culture. They enjoy life. Ulrich Zwingli, for instance, loved music, and many early Calvinists adored poetry. Part of John Calvin's remuneration came in the form of wine. Calvinists entertain, write, and travel; they watch films, pursue political careers, and smoke cigars. Calvinists believe a Christian can serve in the military. They see no inconsistency in this. In fact, 16th-century French Calvinists went to war against French Catholics, and believed they were serving God when they did.

LES
PSEAVMES
MIS EN RIME
FRANCOISE
Par Clement Marot, & Theodore de Beze.
PSAVME IX.

Chantez au Seigneur qui habite en Sion, &
anoncez ses faicts entre les peuples.

Par Iean Bonnefoy.
1 5 6 3.
Auec priuilege.

7. The Genevan Psalter. The complete translation with musical
accompaniment was accomplished in 1562.

They used the Psalms, which had been arranged metrically and set to tunes, as part of their preparation for war, singing them on their way into battle (Figure 7).

Perseverance

This teaching of Calvinism is represented by the P in the TULIP acronym, Perseverance of the Saints (here 'saints' simply means Christians). The work of special grace is permanent, which means the convert will never fall away; she will never leave Christianity. Yet there are at least three apparent problems with this teaching.

The first is based on experience. The evidence of everyday life tells us that many people turn away from Christianity. They become atheists, or agnostics, or Buddhists. Even Christian ministers do this.

The second problem is that the Bible is replete with warnings about falling away. 'Therefore let him who thinks he stands take heed that he does not fall' (1 Corinthians 10:11–12). If, in fact, a person cannot fall, then surely these warnings would seem to be superfluous and potentially harmful.

Third, the Bible speaks plainly about people actually falling away. Hebrews 6 describes someone who has fallen away, and explains that 'it is impossible for those who' have once been enlightened, tasted the heavenly gift, shared in the Holy Spirit, and so forth 'to be brought back to repentance', if they 'fall away'.

Calvinism takes the view that none of these apparent problems is actually real. According to Calvinism, once God has predestined someone, he does not change his mind. Nothing about a converted Christian can possibly surprise God. God already knows how sinful they are. Calvinists acknowledge that true Christians can, and do, sin frequently and often grievously. As John Owen, the English Puritan, said of the sin that dwells in every Christian:

'Your enemy is not only *upon* you... but is *in* you also.' Calvinism also notes that Jesus, being fully cognizant of such facts, promised to take care of everyone whom his Father 'has given me' so that, Jesus says, 'I lose none of them, but raise them up on the last day' (John 6:39; 10:27).

So, the question to ask is, what does God's purpose and Christ's care for his people look like? Can this purpose and care fail? Calvinism teaches they cannot.

God's purpose and care guarantee that the spiritual life of the Christian is never snuffed out. Even when Christians sin, they do not lose the spiritual life (or nature) that burns like a candle within them. The Holy Spirit maintains their faith. Though it may weaken with repeated sinning, it still burns in their breast.

Another aspect of this purpose and care is ensuring that the Christian continues in their spiritual walk. The Reformed faith teaches that the sinning Christian will always repent, return to God, and ask forgiveness. This enduring is vital. Scripture declares 'whoever endures to the end will be saved' (Matthew 10:22). The true Christian will endure. For this, the Reformed point to Philippians 1:6: God 'who began a good work in you will carry it on to completion until the day of Christ Jesus'. If he promises he will carry it on to completion, then he will.

Neither of these points are true of the false convert. There are people who seem to, but do not really, convert to Christianity. They may have a genuine interest in the gospel. They may attend church and taste of the good things of God. They may learn a large amount about Jesus and the Bible. But despite all of this, they are not true converts. They do not have faith burning in their hearts and they will, at some point, fall away.

The points found in the last few paragraphs explain how Calvinists understand the first and third problems mentioned earlier. They understand Hebrews 6 to be speaking about a false convert. False converts may, in fact, have a strong interest in Christianity for some time, but they never experience God's converting work brought about through his special grace. So, as is explained in 1 John 2:19, false converts eventually make themselves known: 'They went out from us, but they did not really belong to us. For if they had belonged to us, they would have remained with us; but they went out, so that it would be shown that they were not of us.' But it remains to explain the second problem. What does the Calvinist do with biblical warnings about falling away?

The Reformed note that all the scriptural passages (Mark 4:16–18; 1 Corinthians 10:11–12; Romans 15:4; James 1:14–16, etc.) which warn of the dangers of falling away (i.e. leaving the Christian faith) imply that believers *can* fall away. Because of this, those who object to the Reformed teaching conclude perseverance is a false doctrine. After all, it teaches that Christians cannot fall away, but the Bible says they can.

Against this incorrect conclusion, Calvinists explain that if the Christian is depending on herself, then she certainly *can* fall away. But, they further elaborate, that does not overturn the doctrine of perseverance, because this doctrine does *not* teach a robotic Christian assurance. It does not assert that believers are immunized against losing their faith in the way that, for instance, a computer is incapable of catching a cold.

Rather, Calvinism teaches that the certainty a Christian possesses that she will never fall away does not arise from her own inability to fall away but from God the Father's predestining purpose, the Spirit's sealing and protecting, and Christ's promise that he will not lose her. This, Calvinism insists, is the repository of the Christian's assurance and perseverance.

Calvinism explains that God, in order to pursue this aim, uses means that appeal to the believer's intellect, will, and free agency.

And one of the means God employs to ensure that the Christian does not fall away is the warning (found in various places in the Bible) of the real danger of doing so. These warnings achieve their intended aim precisely because, when the true Christian reads them, she feels profoundly her own weakness and liability to the slightest temptation and, because she feels these things, she turns to God in prayer, reads her Bible, and so forth—and through these means, she is strengthened in her faith and perseveres.

So, Calvinists deny that these biblical warnings imply the real possibility of a true Christian *actually* falling away, seeing them instead as part of the means God uses to ensure she never will. If someone protests that this is a precarious and nerve-racking assurance, the Calvinist denies the accusation. In fact, the Calvinist retorts, the believer's confidence is sure and unwavering precisely because it rests on the efforts of someone who is omnipotent and has promised never to fail them.

Chapter 8
God and hell

Jonathan Edwards wrote *The End for which God Created the World*, which was republished by John Piper in 2006. Many have pondered this question, but let us attend to the speculations of Edwards for a moment.

Edwards argues that God's aim in creating the world is his own glory. This probably strikes us as rather arrogant, more than a little bit odd, and perhaps quite unflattering. After all, we are taught that it is wrong to be self-centred. And even though Edwards goes on to say that God's pursuit of his own glory actually works ultimately to the benefit of God's people (i.e. the church), we may still be left wondering at the character of this God.

Behind his speculations we find a certain vision of God. God's pursuit of his own glory involves him in certain things. It involves him, for instance, in working to bring his elect to heaven. This, according to Edwards and other Calvinists too, reveals God's kindness, mercy, and love, which he has lavished on his people by bringing them to be with him for eternity.

Other aspects of this divine pursuit involve the revealing of God's various perfections to his elect. Edwards preached a series of sermons on 1 Corinthians 13 in which he explained that heaven will be a world of love. There God will wipe away every tear. He will show his love to them in ways the Bible says no one can imagine. These things will be part of God's endeavour to glorify himself.

Part of what God will reveal includes his justice. God's pursuit of his own glory will, therefore—so say Edwards and other Calvinists—entail God revealing his justice to the elect through his punishing of sinners. Those categorized as 'sinners' or 'the wicked' are any who were not converted to Christianity. They will suffer eternally in hell. And lest we miss the point, this was part of God's original design. It was planned by God before he began to create that he would punish the wicked in eternal torment in order to reveal his own glory to his elect.

This may come as a shock. Hell is an idea that the average reader of *Der Spiegel* or *reddit* finds extremely difficult to make sense of. Divine retribution seems archaic; eternal punishment immoral. It is difficult for many today to conceive of God doing this: not only creating a place like hell, but designing it for the purpose of revealing his own glory through punishing human beings in such a place.

Yet according to Edwards and other Calvinists, hell is part of God's design. In fact, the doctrine of hell has recently been defended quite vigorously by Calvinists. Some of the great Reformed discussions of the doctrine include John Bunyan's *A Few Sighs and Groans from Hell* and W. G. T. Shedd's *The Doctrine of Endless Punishment*, but more recent defences of it are not hard to find. When, in the late 20th century, some conservative Christians began to introduce the possibility that hell would not involve eternal suffering but rather merely the complete annihilation of the sinner, Calvinists like Pittsburgh Theological Seminary professor, John Gerstner, responded by writing *Repent or Perish: The Conservative Attack on Hell*, which defends the traditional doctrine. Other Calvinists too—Arthur Pink, R. C. Sproul, John MacArthur, and John Piper—have all popped up in the 20th and 21st centuries to defend the doctrine.

Being part of God's design, Edwards teaches that hell is something Christians will rejoice over. He and other Calvinists teach that the elect in heaven will not only be able actually to see the wicked suffering but will be glad at the sight (they believe this is taught in texts like Luke 16:19–31, which is the story of the rich man and Lazarus). The basic point Edwards makes to support this assertion is that Christians in heaven cannot possibly be sad or feel grief, since such feelings would be 'inconsistent with that state of perfect happiness' which all those in heaven will experience. Instead of being sad, Christians will rejoice in the perfect justice of God exhibited before them in his punishing of wrongdoing (i.e. the wicked). Not all Calvinists concur with this position, but many do.

Such considerations highlight the strangeness, or otherness, of this Calvinist vision. The idea of otherness is fairly common when discussing conceptions of God throughout history. It is not unique to Calvinism. Rudolph Otto, the 19th-century German Lutheran, spoke of God in these terms, identifying what he called the 'terrifying mystery' (*mysterium tremendum*, as he referred to it in Latin) and explaining it as a 'non-rational, non-sensory experience or feeling whose primary and immediate object is outside the self'. His thought draws on older sources. Thomas Aquinas, the great medieval Catholic theologian, said that God was *sui generis*; that is, of its own kind. Likewise, going back further still, Augustine spoke about the light of the Lord appearing to him in his mind and being fundamentally different. 'This light was...exceedingly different from all other lights.' In speaking like this, he was putting his finger on the idea of divine otherness. But, while fairly common throughout Christian thinking on God, it finds powerful expression within Calvinism, as the reflections of Edwards on God's pursuit of his own glory demonstrate.

Calvinism contends that the Christian must respond to this otherness with trust. God's ways of acting must take priority such that they act as a corrective to the believer. On the doctrine of hell, for instance, Augustine comes in handy again. He sets out how this vision of God corrects impoverished human mental capacities. Acknowledging that hell seems harsh and unjust, he explains:

> Eternal punishment seems hard and unjust to human perceptions, because in the weakness of our mortal condition there is wanting that highest and purest wisdom by which it can be perceived how great a wickedness was committed in that first transgression.

Calvinism wholeheartedly concurs with this Augustinian sentiment. A clash between human perceptions and God's truth means there's a problem with *human* perceptions, which need to be brought into line with God's perceptions.

This trust also recognizes in God's ways something not only different but higher than human capacities. So, John Calvin explains that when we talk about the knowledge the Christian has of God, 'we do not mean comprehension of the sort that is commonly concerned with those things that fall under human sense perception'. Rather, it is 'so far above sense that the human mind has to go beyond and rise above itself in order to attain it'. Continuing in this discussion (which is from his *Institutes*), Calvin explains that what the Christian sees is 'in every way infinite'. He says this kind of knowledge is 'far more lofty than all understanding'.

But concerning the issue of trust, the question is raised by some in relation to Christianity: how can a person trust a God who can send someone to hell? And, of course, that question is more emphatic when directed at the Calvinist, because of the Reformed doctrine of predestination. For the Calvinist asks people to trust a God who can predestine them to hell such that they were created by God for no other reason. God, Calvinism teaches, effectively created some human beings for the ultimate end of suffering eternally in hell for the greater glory of God. How, some say, can a person trust *this* God?

To this, the Calvinist acknowledges that the pull and tug of one's emotions is extraordinary and potentially very difficult, but he ultimately responds, 'I can do nothing else'. For the Reformed, the vision of God compels love and trust. This trust does not blindfold the believer. John Calvin was, for instance, willing to look at God's decree of reprobation and eternal punishment and call it a 'horrible decree'. And yet, that did not stop him or any other Calvinist from believing it or from trusting the God described in scripture. This is the effect this vision of God has.

This reminds us that there is a deep sense of self-abandonment that operates in Calvinist theology. It is a conviction which says that it is right that God should determine the fate of every human being. Who else could do it better? Therefore, no human may stand in a position to judge God or God's decisions. To the Calvinist, this vision of God is ravishing and all-consuming, even if to the world it is confusing.

Hell and the God of love

But these reflections raise an extremely important question. In the simplest form, the question is: isn't God love (as the Bible says, 1 John 4:8)? If this is so, then a further series of questions seem inescapable. Why doesn't God save everyone? Why doesn't he covenant with the entire human race, predestining everyone to eternal salvation? Why didn't God stop the fall of Adam and Eve from occurring? If God is love, how can he reprobate some to eternal damnation?

We could attempt to answer these questions—specifically the question about why, according to Calvinism, God doesn't save everyone—in different ways, but I want to begin to address that specific question by taking up a recent criticism of Calvinism that helpfully explores it and will allow us to say more about Reformed thinking on God.

The criticism seeks to expose Calvinism as internally incoherent. It was made by a philosopher named Jerry Walls, a professor at Houston Baptist University. He wrote (together with Joseph Dongell) *Why I am not a Calvinist* and has also produced a popular YouTube video entitled, 'What's Wrong with Calvinism'. By considering his criticism, we will be able to explore more deeply Calvinist understandings of God's love and of hell.

Walls seeks to show that if Calvinists were consistent in their beliefs, they would have no option but to believe that God is going to save every single human being. And yet, they don't believe this. Hence, Calvinism is inconsistent.

Walls calls his argument the Calvinist Conundrum. Setting it out, Walls first outlines five premises. Four of these summarize Calvinist beliefs about divine love and salvation, and the fifth draws what Walls feels is the unavoidable conclusion to which these beliefs lead. I will set them out the way Walls does:

1. God truly loves all persons.
2. Truly to love someone is to desire their well-being and to promote their true flourishing as much as you can.
3. The well-being and true flourishing of all persons is to be found in a right relationship with God, a saving relationship in which we love and obey him.
4. God could determine all persons freely to accept a right relationship with himself and be saved.
5. Therefore, all will be saved.

Walls explains that almost all Calvinists deny premise 5. He then notes that in order to deny that premise, they must logically also deny one of the other premises. It is in deciding which one to deny

116

that Walls establishes his critique of Calvinism, which rests on the fact that Calvinists cannot find one of the other premises which they feel comfortable denying. Hence, the conundrum.

How does Reformed theology respond to this critique and what do their responses teach us about the Reformed vision of God and his love? Their responses vary. I will consider two.

First, as Walls himself mentions, there are Reformed theologians who deny that God loves all persons (premise 1). Arthur Pink, the English Calvinist who died in 1952, is one such theologian, but others could be mentioned. This response tends to highlight the covenant love that God has solely for his elect—a love which ensures the well-being of the elect. Theologians like Pink also point out, in defence of their position, that there are biblical passages that seem to limit divine love. Psalm 11:5 states: 'The LORD examines the righteous, but the wicked, those who love violence, he hates with a passion.' Psalm 5:4–5 says something similar. So, for anyone who is willing (like Pink) to deny the first premise, there is no conundrum.

Second, there are Calvinists who accept premises 1 through 4, but still extract themselves from this conundrum by arguing that Walls has misrepresented Reformed beliefs on God's love. These Calvinists contend that his four premises leave out something essential to a right understanding of God's love for humankind. There is, they argue, need for another premise to be added, which would correct the error in his argument (i.e. it would allow someone to embrace premises 1 to 4 without concluding premise 5) and answer the challenge Walls presents to Calvinism. This additional premise focuses on God's wisdom.

In his argument, Walls is essentially saying: 'if you say that God loves everyone and that he could save everyone, then you have a problem, since you are not a universalist. And this is precisely what Reformed theology says. So it has a problem.' We can find a

Calvinist articulating similar points but handling them so as to
draw a very different conclusion if we look to Robert Lewis
Dabney, the American Presbyterian who died in 1898.

In his *Systematic Theology*, Dabney declared: 'God says in His
Word that He has compassion on lost sinners. He says that He
could save if He wished.' These are premises 1 through 4 in a
nutshell. But to them Dabney added:

> His word and providence both show us that some are permitted to
> be lost. In a wise and good man, we can easily understand how a
> power to pardon, a sincere compassion for a guilty criminal, and yet
> a fixed purpose to punish, could coexist; the power and compassion
> being overruled by his wisdom. Why may not something analogous
> take place in God, according to His unchanging nature?

Here Dabney delineates what we might call premise 4b, which
concerns the fact that God's wisdom sometimes overrules (so to
speak) his compassion and his power. In adding this to his
reflections on the question, Dabney resolves the conundrum
which Walls claims plagues Calvinism, leaving himself and other
Calvinists to deny premise 5 without any problem.

Dabney's negotiating of the problem reveals something important
about Calvinism, namely, that it believes the inscrutability
of God's wisdom to be an absolutely basic biblical tenet (Job
11:7, 38–42; Isaiah 55:8–9; Romans 11:33). God's choices, even
when considered within the context of contemplating divine love,
simply cannot always be understood perfectly by human beings.
But Walls (apparently) does not agree with this. His criticism of
Calvinism is predicated on the idea that humans can *always*
understand God's decisions. To this, Dabney and the entire
Reformed tradition say: 'It is exceeding presumption to
suppose that, because we do not see such a cause, none can
be known to God.'

Now, does this line of argument actually require the Calvinist to bite the bullet and agree with Arthur Pink that God simply does not love every single human soul? Does it require her to deny that 'God is love', as is stated in 1 John 4:8? Not according to Dabney. It merely requires her to believe other biblical statements too, such as: 'Who has known the mind of the Lord so as to instruct him?' (1 Corinthians 2:16).

The number of the elect

So, we have considered Calvinism's fixation with hell and divine otherness and we've noted how incomprehensible it thinks God's love is. Is there anything positive it has to say about God?

For this, we turn to Reformed thinking on the number of the elect. Until approximately 120 years ago, Calvinism, not to mention essentially the entire Western Christian tradition, believed that the number of people whom God had elected to salvation was small. In the late 19th century, this belief changed among an important segment of the Reformed community.

B. B. Warfield, who taught at Princeton Seminary until 1921 and was one of the leading Presbyterian theologians of his era, was one of those who produced a new answer to the question of the number of the elect. Warfield raised the topic explicitly, and argued that biblical passages commonly used to support a small elect (like Luke 13:22–30) do not teach that. Further, he contended that the teaching of scripture is that the elect will be 'as numerous as the stars in the sky and as the sand on the seashore', citing God's promise to Abraham in Genesis 22:17. Given Warfield's authority within the Reformed tradition, his challenge has carried significant weight and had a lasting legacy within the tradition. Warfield's challenge was, in fact, anticipated in the theological reflections of one of his equally important contemporaries, Abraham Kuyper.

Their reflections focus our attention on this basic question—what, according to Calvinism, are God's loving plans for the race of humans which he has placed on this earth? Asked in a more specific manner, we might probe *again*—because we have already considered aspects of it in Chapters 2 and 3—what Calvinists think of biblical assertions that God is going to save 'the world'; assertions such as: 'For God did not send his Son into the world to condemn the world, but that the world might be saved through Him' (John 3:17). What does the Calvinist make of such a statement? After all, when Calvinists sing from the Psalter of the Free Church of Scotland, they sing the words of Psalm 72:

> Yea, all the mighty kings of earth
> Before him down shall fall;
> And all the nations of the world
> Do service to him shall.

But what do they mean when they sing this? Do they have in mind the idea that the nations of the world are serving God because God saved them and brought them into fellowship with him? Does Calvinism, in other words, possibly understand God's saving will as including the majority of the human race; as entailing something approaching an idea closer to the 'world'?

On these questions there is no unanimity among Calvinists, even if we restrict ourselves to a specific time period or geographical location. But, for the likes of Warfield and Kuyper, these queries are answered *optimistically*. I have already indicated that Warfield argued against the once-standard reading of passages like Luke 13:22–30 and the idea of a small elect. His defence of a large elect addresses specifically the loving purposes of God. In a sermon on John 3:16–17, Warfield urged that, 'Surely, we shall not wish to measure the saving work of God by what has been already accomplished.' He reminded his hearers: 'Are not the saints to inherit the earth? Is not the re-created earth theirs?' And in

Warfield's article 'Are They Few that be Saved?' he quoted Kuyper approvingly:

> If we liken mankind, thus, as it has grown up out of Adam, to a tree,
> then the elect are not leaves which have been plucked off from the
> tree, that there may be braided from them a wreath for God's glory,
> while the tree itself is to be felled, rooted up and cast into the fire;
> but precisely the contrary, the lost are the branches, twigs and
> leaves which have fallen away from the stem of mankind, while the
> elect alone remain attached to it.

Whether this squares with what Edwards said about God's end for creating is an interesting question. My hunch is probably not. But disagreement is nothing new to Calvinism. Besides, there's something sensible, profound, and even (I might say) beautiful about Kuyper's articulation. Warfield also cites a number of others who agree with him and Kuyper, including Alvah Hovey, W. G. T. Shedd, Charles Hodge, and Robert Lewis Dabney. Not a bad public, that.

Chronology

1515-16   Johannes Oecolampadius becomes cathedral preacher at Basel. A year later Desiderius Erasmus publishes his Greek New Testament and Erasmus and Ulrich Zwingli meet in Basel.

1523   Zwingli engages in two public disputations (formal debates) with Catholic theologians.

1525   On 11 April, a group including Zwingli, Leo Jud, and Oswald Myconius successfully petition the Zurich council to abolish the Catholic mass.

1529   Introduction of Reformation in Basel.

1536   John Calvin, author of the *Institutes of the Christian Religion*, arrives in Geneva and is persuaded to stay by Guillaume Farel.

1538   Debrecen Reformed College is established in Debrecen, Hungary.

1556   John Łaski travels back to Poland, becoming secretary to King Sigismund II and bringing Reformed theology to the country.

1559   Frederick III, ruler of the Palatinate, takes office, making that portion of Germany Calvinist with the imposing of the *Heidelberg Catechism*.

1562   In spring of this year, the first of the French Wars of Religion begins between the Calvinist Huguenots and the Catholic armies of France.

1566	Heinrich Bullinger publishes his *Second Helvetic Confession of Faith*.
1578	The *Second Book of Discipline* is adopted in Scotland.
1618–19	In the Netherlands, the Synod of Dordt rejects the teachings of Jacob Arminius.
1620	The Pilgrims arrive in New Plymouth in North America.
1630	Puritans establish the Massachusetts Bay Colony.
1642	In England, the parliament meets in Westminster Abbey to produce a new order for the church.
1652	Jan van Riebeeck establishes an outpost at the Cape of Good Hope, which eventually brings (primarily) Dutch settlers and Calvinism.
1678	In February of this year the English Baptist, John Bunyan, publishes *The Pilgrim's Progress*.
1702	Cotton Mather publishes *Magnalia Christi Americana*, which recounts the religious history of the colonies in New England from 1620 to 1698.
1718	Edward Fisher's *The Marrow of Modern Divinity* is republished, prompting the Marrow Controversy.
1741	On 8 July, Jonathan Edwards preaches 'Sinners in the Hands of an Angry God' in Enfield, Connecticut.
1792-6	Andrew Fuller founds the Baptist Missionary Society. Also London Missionary Society and Edinburgh Missionary Society are founded.
1812	Princeton Theological Seminary is founded.
1830	Alexander Duff, a Reformed missionary, arrives in Calcutta.
1843	The Free Church of Scotland is formed after the Disruption from the Church of Scotland, led by David Welsh and Thomas Chalmers. New College, now part of Edinburgh University, is established.
1847	The Evangelical Presbyterian Church of Ghana is founded.
1853	Presbyterian missionary, John Nevius, sails from America to China.
1854	Charles Spurgeon, converted four years earlier at a Primitive Methodist chapel, becomes pastor of New Park Street Chapel in London.

1859	The first presbytery in Brazil is established by American missionary, Ashbel Green Simonton.
1892	Abraham Kuyper's Reformed Church of the Netherlands is established.
1898	Abraham Kuyper delivers the Stone Lectures at Princeton Theological Seminary which are published as *Lectures on Calvinism*.
1912	The first General Assembly is held by Presbyterians in Korea.
1929	J. Gresham Machen leaves Princeton Theological Seminary to found Westminster Theological Seminary.
1934	Swiss theologians, Karl Barth and Emil Brunner, debate the possibility and status of natural theology.
1936	The Orthodox Presbyterian Church is established in the United States of America.
1937	Hyung-Nong Park translates Loraine Boettner's *The Reformed Doctrine of Predestination* into Korean.
1938	D. Martyn Lloyd-Jones, born in Cardiff, Wales, is appointed as associate pastor of Westminster Chapel in London.
1948	Apartheid is established in South Africa, both defended and condemned by Reformed theologians.
1957	The Banner of Truth Trust is established by Iain Murray in Scotland.
1959	The Hapdong Presbyterian Church is formed in Korea through the leadership of Hyung-Nong Park.
1989	Tim Keller founds Redeemer Presbyterian Church in New York.
1994	John Piper and Jon Bloom found Desiring God Ministries.
2009	*Time* magazine lists 'The New Calvinism' as one of the ten ideas changing the world at that time.

Further reading

Websites

English works
Various authors (old translations) available at <http://www.ccel.org/>.

Latin, French, and German works
Older authors available at <http://www.e-rara.ch> or <http://www.prdl.org>.

Zwingli, Bullinger, and Calvin studies
Zwingli, see: <http://www.irg.uzh.ch/static/zwingli-werke/index.php>.
Bullinger, see: <http://www.irg.uzh.ch/de/hbbw/baende.html>.
Calvin, see: <http://www.archive-ouverte.unige.ch/unige:650>.

Kuyper's works
<http://www.abrahamkuyper.com>.

Zwingli, Bullinger, and Zurich

Heinrich Bullinger, *The Decades of Henry Bullinger,* 2 vols (Grand Rapids, 2004).

Bruce Gordon and Emidio Campi (eds), *Architect of Reformation: An Introduction to Heinrich Bullinger, 1504–1575* (Grand Rapids, 2004).

Bruce Gordon, *The Swiss Reformation* (Manchester, 2002). Careful and insightful historical analysis.

G. R. Potter, *Zwingli* (Cambridge, 1976).

W. P. Stephen, *The Theology of Huldrych Zwingli* (New York, 1986). Clear explanation of themes in Zwingli's thought.

Ulrich Zwingli, *Commentary on True and False Religion* (Philadelphia, 1981).

Calvin and Geneva

Jon Balserak, *John Calvin as Sixteenth-Century Prophet* (Oxford, 2014). Examination of Calvin's sense of vocation.

William Bouwsma, *John Calvin: A Sixteenth-Century Portrait* (Oxford, 1988). Important reading of Calvin's life and thought.

John Calvin, *Institutes of the Christian Religion*, 2 vols (Philadelphia, 1960).

Bruce Gordon, *Calvin* (New Haven, 2009). Best one-volume biography of Calvin.

Robert Kingdon, *Reforming Geneva: Discipline, Faith and Anger in Calvin's Geneva* (Geneva, 2012).

Herman Selderhuis (ed.), *The Calvin Handbook* (Grand Rapids, 2009).

History of Calvinism

Philip Benedict, *Christ's Churches Purely Reformed: A Social History of Calvinism* (New Haven, 2002). Standard work on the rise and development of Calvinism; replaces J. T. McNeill's older study.

D. G. Hart, *Calvinism: A History* (New Haven, 2013).

Richard Muller, *Post-Reformation Reformed Dogmatics ca. 1520 to ca. 1725*, 4 vols (Grand Rapids, 2003). Standard work on the first two centuries of Reformed thought.

Classic interpretations

Loraine Boettner, *The Reformed Doctrine of Predestination* (New York, 2012).

Abraham Kuyper, *Lectures on Calvinism* (New York, 2007). Extremely influential articulation of Neo-Calvinist thought.

Arthur W. Pink, *The Sovereignty of God* (Grand Rapids, 1994).

Cornelius Van Til, *The Defense of the Faith* (Phillipsburg, NJ, 2008).

Geerhardus Vos, *Biblical Theology: Old and New Testaments* (Grand Rapids, 1959). Brilliant exposition of the Redemptive-historical approach to theology.

Max Weber, *The Protestant Ethic and the Spirit of Capitalism* (Routledge, 2001). Justly-famous and still engaging essay on the interaction between religious ideas and economics.

Jerome Zanchi, *Absolute Predestination* (Grand Rapids, 1977).

Five points/introductions to Calvinism

Willem van Asselt, *Introduction to Reformed Scholasticism* (Grand Rapids, 2011).

William Edgar, *Truth in all its Glory: Commending the Reformed Faith* (Grand Rapids, 2012).

Richard Mouw, *Calvinism in the Las Vegas Airport: Making Connections in Today's World* (Grand Rapids, 2004). Excellent accessible introduction to Calvinism.

Charles Spurgeon, *A Defence of Calvinism* (Carlisle, PA, 2010). Impassioned defence of themes central to Calvinism.

David Steele and Curtis Thomas, *The Five Points of Calvinism: Defined, Defended and Documented* (Phillipsburg, NJ, 1963).

Culture

Richard Mouw, *The Challenges of Cultural Discipleship: Essays in the Line of Abraham Kuyper* (Grand Rapids, 2011).

H. Richard Niebuhr, *Christ and Culture* (New York, 2002). The classic treatment.

Cornelius J. Plantinga, *Engaging God's World: A Christian Vision of Faith, Learning, and Living* (Grand Rapids, 2002).

H. R. Rookmaaker, *Modern Art and the Death of a Culture* (Downers Grove, IL, 1994).

David VanDrunen, *Living in God's Two Kingdoms: A Biblical Vision for Christianity and Culture* (Wheaton, 2010).

Henry Van Til, *Calvinistic Concept of Culture* (Baker, 1959). Engaging exposition of Reformed view of culture.

Albert Wolters, *Creation Regained: Biblical Basics for a Reformational Worldview* (Grand Rapids, 2005).

Calvinist theologies

Karl Barth, *Church Dogmatics*, 14 vols (Peabody, MA, 2010).

Herman Bavinck, *Reformed Dogmatics*, 4 vols (Grand Rapids, 2008).

G. C. Berkouwer, *Studies in Dogmatics*, 14 vols (Grand Rapids, 1981).

Robert Lewis Dabney, *Systematic Theology* (Carlisle, PA, 1985). Best one-volume exposition of Reformed theology.

Jonathan Edwards, *The Works of Jonathan Edwards*, 2 vols (Edinburgh, 1974). Contains many of his major writings.

Patrick Fairbairn, *The Typology of Scripture* (Grand Rapids, 2000).

Edward Fisher, *The Marrow of Modern Divinity* (Fearn, UK, 2009).

Wayne Grudem, *Systematic Theology: An Introduction to Biblical Doctrine* (Grand Rapids, 1994).

Heinrich Heppe, *Reformed Dogmatics* (Eugene, 2008).

Francis Turretin, *Institutes of Elenctic Theology*, 3 vols (Phillipsburg, NJ, 1992–7). Extremely influential.

Geerhardus Vos, *Pauline Eschatology* (Grand Rapids, 1979).

Apologetics/defence of Christianity

John Hartung, *Truth in the Flesh* (Chipley, FL, 2012).

J. Gresham Machen, *Christianity and Liberalism* (Grand Rapids, 2009).

Cornelius Van Til and Greg L. Bahnsen (eds), *Van Til's Apologetic: Readings and Analysis* (Grand Rapids, 1998).

Reformed confessions

Joel Beeke and Sinclair Ferguson (eds), *Reformed Confessions Harmonized* (Grand Rapids, 1999). Very useful synthesis.

James T. Dennison Jr (ed.), *Reformed Confessions of the 16th and 17th Centuries in English Translation: (1523–1693)*, 4 vols (Grand Rapids, 2014).

Impact of Calvinism

Irena Backus and Philip Benedict, *Calvin and His Influence, 1509–2009* (Oxford, 2011). Superb coverage extending beyond Calvin to Calvinism in Europe, Africa, and America.

Aliki Barnstone, Michael Tomasek Manson, and Carol J. Singley (eds), *The Calvinist Roots of the Modern Era* (Hanover, NH, 1997). Engaging on Calvinism's influence on literature.

Edward Dommen and James D. Bratt (eds), *John Calvin Rediscovered: The Impact of his Social and Economic Thought* (London, 2007).

American Calvinism

Joshua Guthman, *Strangers Below: Primitive Baptists and American Culture* (Chapel Hill, 2015).

D. G. Hart and John R. Muether, *Seeking a Better Country: 300 Years of American Presbyterianism* (Grand Rapids, 2007).

Jacob T. Hoogstra (ed.), *American Calvinism: A Survey* (Grand Rapids, 1957).

David F. Wells, *Reformed Theology in America: A History of Its Modern Development* (Grand Rapids, 1985).

European Calvinism

James Bratt, *Dutch Calvinism in Modern America: A History of a Conservative Subculture* (Grand Rapids, 1984).

Gijsbert van den Brink and Harro M. Höpfl (eds), *Calvinism and the Making of the European Mind* (Leiden, 2014). Engaging collection of wide-ranging essays.

W. Fred Graham (ed.), *Later Calvinism: International Perspectives* (Kirksville, MO, 1994).

R. Po-Chia Hsia, *Calvinism and Religious Toleration in the Dutch Golden Age* (Cambridge, 2010).

Menna Prestwich (ed.), *International Calvinism, 1541–1715* (Oxford, 1985).

British Calvinism

David Ceri Jones, Boyd Stanley Schlenther, and Eryn Mant White, *The Elect Methodists: Calvinistic Methodism in England and Wales, 1735–1811* (Cardiff, 2012).

John MacLeod, *Scottish Theology* (Edinburgh, 1974). A classic text.

Ian Shaw, *High Calvinism in Action: Calvinism and the City, Manchester and London, 1810–1860* (Oxford, 2003).

James Walker, *The Theology and Theologians of Scotland: Chiefly of the Seventeenth and Eighteenth Centuries* (Edinburgh, 1888).

African Calvinism

Allan A. Boesak, *Black and Reformed: Apartheid, Liberation, and the Calvinist Tradition* (Eugene, 1984).

Jonathan Neil Gerstner, *The Thousand Generation Covenant: Dutch Reformed Covenant Theology and Group Identity in Colonial South Africa, 1652–1814* (Leiden, 1991).

Adam Mohr, *Enchanted Calvinism: Labor Migration, Afflicting Spirits, and Christian Therapy in the Presbyterian Church of Ghana* (Rochester, NY, 2013).

Korean/Australian Calvinism

In-Sub Ahn, 'Calvin in Asia', in *The Calvin Handbook* (Grand Rapids, 2009), 512–19.

Sung-Kuh Chung, *Korean Church and Reformed Faith: Focusing on the Historical Study of Preaching in the Korean Church* (Seattle, 1996).

Iain Murray, *Australian Christian Life from 1788: An Introduction and an Anthology* (Carlisle, PA, 1988).

New Calvinism/contemporary debate/Federal Vision

R. Scott Clark, *Recovering the Reformed Confession* (Grand Rapids, 2008).

Oliver Crisp, *Deviant Calvinism: Broadening Reformed Theology* (Fortress, 2014). Excellent reappraisal of the contours of the Reformed tradition.

Collin Hansen, *Young, Restless, Reformed: A Journalist's Journey with the New Calvinists* (Wheaton, 2008). A lively account of the rise of the New Calvinists.

Michael Horton, *For Calvinism* (Zondervan, 2011).

Roger Olson, *Against Calvinism* (Zondervan, 2011).

Robert A. Peterson and Michael D. Williams, *Why I Am Not an Arminian* (Downers Grove, 2004).

John Piper, *God's Passion for His Glory: Living the Vision of Jonathan Edwards* (Wheaton, 1988).

Carl Trueman, *The Creedal Imperative* (Wheaton, 2012).

Jerry L. Walls and Joseph R. Dongell, *Why I Am Not a Calvinist* (Downers Grove, 2004).

Guy Prentiss Waters, *The Federal Vision and Covenant Theology: A Comparative Analysis* (Grand Rapids, 2006).

Steve Wilkins and Duane Garner, *The Federal Vision* (Monroe, 2004).

David F. Wright, *What has Infant Baptism done to Baptism? An Enquiry at the End of Christendom* (Milton Keynes, 2005).

Index

Calvinism

Calvinism

Calvinism

Expand your collection of
VERY SHORT INTRODUCTIONS

PENTECOSTALISM
A Very Short Introduction
William K. Kay

In religious terms Pentecostalism was probably the most
vibrant and rapidly-growing religious movement of the 20th
century. Starting as a revivalistic and renewal movement within
Christianity, it encircled the globe in less than 25 years and
grew in North America and then in those parts of the world
with the highest birth-rates. Characterised by speaking in
tongues, miracles, television evangelism and megachurches, it
is also noted for its small-group meetings, empowerment of
individuals, liberation of women and humanitarian concerns.
William K Kay outlines the origins and growth of
Pentecostalism, looking at not only the theological aspects of
the movement, but also the sociological influences of its
political and humanitarian viewpoints.

www.oup.com/vsi

SCIENCE AND RELIGION
A Very Short Introduction
Thomas Dixon

The debate between science and religion is never out of the news: emotions run high, fuelled by polemical bestsellers and, at the other end of the spectrum, high-profile campaigns to teach 'Intelligent Design' in schools. Yet there is much more to the debate than the clash of these extremes. As Thomas Dixon shows in this balanced and thought-provoking introduction, many have seen harmony rather than conflict between faith and science. He explores not only the key philosophical questions that underlie the debate, but also the social, political, and ethical contexts that have made 'science and religion' such a fraught and interesting topic in the modern world, offering perspectives from non-Christian religions and examples from across the physical, biological, and social sciences.

'A rich introductory text . . . on the study of relations of science and religion.'

R. P. Whaite, Metascience